FROM
Surviving
TO Thriving

Sara Miller McCune founded SAGE Publishing in 1965 to support the dissemination of usable knowledge and educate a global community. SAGE publishes more than 1000 journals and over 800 new books each year, spanning a wide range of subject areas. Our growing selection of library products includes archives, data, case studies and video. SAGE remains majority owned by our founder and after her lifetime will become owned by a charitable trust that secures the company's continued independence.

Los Angeles | London | New Delhi | Singapore | Washington DC | Melbourne

FROM
Surviving
TO Thriving

A student's guide to feeling
and doing well at university

EDITED BY
Christian van Nieuwerburgh
AND Paige Williams

$SAGE

Los Angeles | London | New Delhi
Singapore | Washington DC | Melbourne

Los Angeles | London | New Delhi
Singapore | Washington DC | Melbourne

SAGE Publications Ltd
1 Oliver's Yard
55 City Road
London EC1Y 1SP

SAGE Publications Inc.
2455 Teller Road
Thousand Oaks, California 91320

SAGE Publications India Pvt Ltd
B 1/I 1 Mohan Cooperative Industrial Area
Mathura Road
New Delhi 110 044

SAGE Publications Asia-Pacific Pte Ltd
3 Church Street
#10-04 Samsung Hub
Singapore 049483

Editor: Donna Goddard
Assistant editor: Esmé Carter
Production editor: Prachi Arora
Copyeditor: Sharon Cawood
Proofreader: Thomas Bedford
Indexer: Cathryn Pritchard
Marketing manager: Camille Richmond
Cover design: Wendy Scott
Typeset by: C&M Digitals (P) Ltd, Chennai, India
Printed in the UK

Library of Congress Control Number: 2021944982

British Library Cataloguing in Publication data

A catalogue record for this book is available from
the British Library

ISBN 978-1-5297-4114-8
ISBN 978-1-5297-4113-1 (pbk)
eISBN 978-1-5297-8853-2

At SAGE we take sustainability seriously. Most of our products are printed in the UK using responsibly sourced papers and
boards. When we print overseas we ensure sustainable papers are used as measured by the PREPS grading system. We
undertake an annual audit to monitor our sustainability.

In memory of Arthur J. van Nieuwerburgh and Tsuyu Tsuchida, with love and gratitude. They gave me a chance.

To my wonderful daughters, Olivia and Isabella, who help me to thrive and who I hope will one day experience thriving through university.

Contents

Acknowledgements

Editors' acknowledgements

We owe a huge debt of gratitude to our wonderful colleagues who shared their expertise, insights and knowledge by writing chapters for this book: Robert Biswas-Diener, Rachel Colla, Andrea Giraldez-Hayes, Rona Hart, Aaron Jarden, Rebecca Jarden, Hanna Kampman, Peggy Kern, Tim Lomas, Ana Paula Nacif, Michael Steger and Aneta Tunariu. We are thankful to each of them for their contribution to this book and the part they play in inspiring university students.

Christian's acknowledgements

This has been a very meaningful project for me as I have been part of a university community ever since I started as a first-year undergraduate student at the American University of Beirut (Lebanon) in September 1989. I am grateful to that institution, its faculty and students for preparing me to make the most of a rich journey of lifelong learning and discovery. I would like to particularly note the lasting impact of Jean-Marie Cook, George Khairallah and Salwa Ghaly – all inspiring educators who continued to serve the university and its students during very challenging times. During my many years completing a PhD at the Shakespeare Institute at the University of Birmingham (UK), I was fortunate to be mentored by one of the world's leading scholars in Elizabethan drama, Martin Wiggins. When I returned to university after my PhD to pursue my newfound interest in psychology, I'm fortunate to have been taught by amazing academics such as Ashok Jansari and Tom Dickson. I am grateful to them and the rest of the faculty in the School of Psychology at the University of East London (UK).

In addition to being a student for many years, I have been fortunate to teach at a number of universities. I am grateful to staff and students in the School of Psychology at the University of East London; in the Centre for Coaching and Behavioural Change at Henley Business School of the University of Reading (UK); in the Psychology Department of Anglia Ruskin University (UK); and in the Psychology Department at the University of Bergamo (Italy). Most recently, I have appreciated the warmth, professionalism and passion of colleagues and students at the Royal College of Surgeons in Ireland. I consider it a privilege to have worked alongside colleagues in each of these institutions, and a pleasure to interact with students in person and virtually.

Notably, I met my wonderful co-editor, Paige Williams, in the Centre for Positive Psychology (now the Centre for Wellbeing Science) at the University of Melbourne (Australia). We discovered that we had a shared passion for supporting people to experience wellbeing (rather than just learn about it) during their time at university. It has been a joy to work with Paige, and I am grateful to her for her collegiality, good humour and resilience.

Paige's acknowledgements

University holds a special place in my life despite my somewhat intermittent relationship with it. As Christian was beginning his university career in Lebanon, I began mine at the University of Portsmouth in the UK, where I completed an honours degree in Business. I am grateful for that experience – quite unique at the time – as it blended learning with a year in industry and provided me with a rich and valuable foundation that launched my corporate career. I did not return to university for nearly 20 years, as work, travel and life more generally kept me busy. When I did, it was to follow an interest generated from my workplace leadership roles in understanding how to create and sustain change. I see now that this distance-learning graduate diploma experience was me 'dipping my toe' back into the waters of university-level learning to see how it felt. The rest as they say is history, as that experience opened me up to the possibility of further study and ultimately my PhD in the Center for Wellbeing Science at the University of Melbourne (Australia). Here, I was fortunate enough to be one of the first PhDs to graduate from the Centre, under the generous and wise supervision of Lea Waters OAM and Peggy Kern. I am grateful to them and the rest of the faculty at the Centre for Wellbeing Science for their care, support and guidance as I completed my PhD.

My experience as a student at university was joyful and expansive, but pales into comparison with my experience of teaching there. I have been fortunate to design, develop and teach a variety of undergraduate and graduate programmes in wellbeing science and change, and have seen the impact of translating cutting-edge research into practical, applied learning that students can build into their everyday lives. I am most grateful to Lindsay Oades, Director of the Centre for Wellbeing Science, for giving me the opportunity and latitude to design and develop these programmes, and to Aaron Jarden for his support in delivering them.

Finally, I would like to thank my co-editor Christian van Nieuwerburgh for his warmth, generosity and commitment as we edited this book; it has transformed what could have been challenging and onerous, into a work of ease and grace. Thank you.

About the authors

Editors

Christian van Nieuwerburgh is Professor of Coaching and Positive Psychology at the Royal College of Surgeons in Ireland and Global Director of Growth Coaching International. He is a well-published author in the fields of coaching and positive psychology with particular interest in ideal environments for learning. He completed a BA and an MA in English Literature at the American University of Beirut (Lebanon) before doing a PhD at the Shakespeare Institute of the University of Birmingham (UK) and gaining an MSc in Psychology at the University of East London (UK). He enjoys travel, motorcycling and time with his family.

Paige Williams is an Honorary Fellow of the Centre for Wellbeing Science at the University of Melbourne (Australia), an Associate of Melbourne Business School (Australia) and an international speaker and leadership mentor. Her work in the fields of leadership, cultures and systems of wellbeing has been presented and published internationally. Paige completed a BA (Hons) Business Studies at the University of Portsmouth (UK) and a Graduate Diploma of Change Management at the University of New South Wales (Australia) before doing a PhD at the Centre for Wellbeing Science, University of Melbourne. She enjoys F45, walking on the beach and laughing with her teenage daughters. Find out more about Paige's work at: http://www.drpaigewilliams.com

Contributors

Robert Biswas-Diener is sometimes called the "Indiana Jones of Positive Psychology" because he has conducted research with the Maasai in Kenya, Amish farmers in the USA, Inuit in Greenland, and other far-flung groups. As a researcher, Robert has published more than 70 peer-reviewed articles on topics as wide-ranging as hospitality, happiness, and education. He is author of *The Upside of Your Dark Side*, and other books. Despite these professional accomplishments, it is not "all work and no play" for Robert. He prizes his recreation. Robert draws every day, is a rock climber, and has taken nearly 30 thousand photos of his cats.

Rachel Colla is a lecturer at the University of Melbourne (Australia), where her research focuses on hope and facilitating wellbeing through learning design. She is a dual-recipient of the University of Melbourne teaching excellence awards, recognizing her outstanding achievement in teaching, skill, and imagination in designing and evaluating teaching programs. Rachel completed a Bachelor of Social Science and Masters of Psychology at the Australian Catholic University (Australia). After many years of practice, she came back to study, completing her Masters of Applied Positive Psychology at the University of Melbourne, where she is also completing her PhD. She loves adventure, design, music and family.

Andrea Giraldez-Hayes is an accredited coaching psychologist, supervisor and consultant specialising in arts and creative approaches to positive psychology and coaching psychology. She is the Programme Director of the Masters in Applied Positive Psychology and Coaching Psychology and Clinical Director of the Wellbeing and Psychological Services Clinic at the School of Psychology of the University of East London (UK). Curious and passionate about learning and personal and professional development, Andrea is a person of many talents built throughout 30 years of experience, having worked for universities, education departments, and international organisations in Europe, the UK, and Latin America. She has authored more than fifty books and peer-reviewed papers.

Rona Hart is a lecturer, researcher and author in Applied Positive Psychology and Mindfulness, and is the Course Director of the distance learning postgraduate programme, The Psychology of Kindness and Wellbeing at Work, at the School of Psychology of the University of Sussex. Rona completed a BA and an MA in Education and Sociology at Tel Aviv University (Israel), a Masters in Applied Positive Psychology at the University of East London (UK), and a PhD in Education at King's College London (UK). She has been teaching and writing about Positive Psychology and mindfulness topics for nearly two decades and particularly interested in their applications in work settings.

Aaron Jarden is an Associate Professor at the Melbourne Graduate School of Education of the University of Melbourne (Australia). He is a wellbeing consultant, social entrepreneur, has multiple qualifications in philosophy, computing, education, and psychology, and is a prolific author and presenter. Over his 27-year academic career he has been at 7 different universities, and enjoys travel, reading biographies, and trying new experiences.

Rebecca Jarden is a registered nurse and lecturer, leading the Intensive Care Nursing course, University of Melbourne (Australia), and a Nursing Research Fellow, Austin Health, Melbourne (Australia). Rebecca studied psychology and anthropology in a BA, DipGrad, University of Otago, a BHSc (Nursing), AUT University

(New Zealand), and post-graduate nursing certificates at Thames Valley University (UK) and Victoria University of Wellington (New Zealand). Rebecca completed her MNursing at Victoria University, then investigated nurse wellbeing in her PhD at AUT University. Her post-doctoral research continues to focus on the health workforce, exploring wellbeing during transition and beyond. Rebecca enjoys time with family/friends, exploring new places, food, art and music.

Hanna Kampman is an enthusiastic happiness intervention from Lapland. She works as a senior lecturer and module leader in the Masters in Applied Positive Psychology and Coaching Psychology programme at the University of East London (UK). She achieved her bachelor's degree in sports and leisure from Lapland University of Applied Sciences (Finland). She moved to London to study her Masters in Applied Positive Psychology at University of East London, where she also completed her PhD. Her love for nature and moving is deeply rooted in the forests and lakes of Lapland, and it is where you will likely find her in her free time.

Peggy Kern is an Associate Professor at the Centre for Wellbeing Science within the Graduate School of Education at the University of Melbourne (Australia). Originally trained in social, personality, and developmental psychology, Peggy received her undergraduate degree in psychology from Arizona State University (US), a Masters and Ph.D. in social/personality psychology from the University of California (US) and postdoctoral training in positive psychology at the University of Pennsylvania (US). Her research focuses on understanding, measuring, and supporting wellbeing across the lifespan. She supports her own wellbeing through running, cycling, and spending time outdoors. You can find out more about Peggy's work at www.peggykern.org.

Tim Lomas is a Psychology Research Scientist at the Harvard T.H. Chan School of Public Health and the Human Flourishing Program at Harvard University (US). Before that he was a lecturer in positive psychology at the University of East London (UK) from 2013-2020. Tim's main research focus is exploring cross-cultural perspectives on wellbeing, such as his lexicography of 'untranslatable' words (www.drtimlomas.com/lexicography). Tim completed an MA and MSc at the University of Edinburgh (UK) and spent six years working as a musician and psychiatric nursing assistant before undertaking his PhD at the University of Westminster (UK) from 2008 to 2012 (exploring the impact of meditation on men's mental health). Tim's passions include music, football, and above all spending time with his family, including new daughter Laila Grace!

Ana Paula Nacif is a lecturer on the Masters of Applied Positive Psychology and Coaching Psychology at the University of East London (UK). Ana is an experienced executive and group coach, facilitator and consultant whose work is focused on wellbeing and leadership. Ana completed a BA in journalism at Universidade Metodista (Brazil). She studied for a Masters in Coaching Psychology at University of East London and gained a professional doctorate in coaching with Oxford Brookes University (UK). She is co-editor of the Philosophy of Coaching Journal. Ana lives in Kent, UK, with her husband, two children and a dog. She loves travelling and exploring new cultures.

Michael F. Steger is Professor of Psychology and the Founding Director for the *Center for Meaning and Purpose* at Colorado State University. He is an internationally recognized authority on the benefits of finding meaning in one's life and in one's work. Michael is a sought after speaker and enjoys providing keynotes, workshops, and retreats around the world on topics ranging from meaning and purpose, flourishing at work, positive education, effective leadership, and expanding clinical practice by incorporating meaning and purpose assessment and interventions.

Aneta D. Tunariu is Professor of Applied Psychology and Chartered Psychologist with the British Psychological Society. Her academic expertise, applied practice, and research are informed by existential philosophy and positive psychology coaching. Aneta gained her BSc (Hons) in Psychology at London South Bank University (UK) in 1999. In the same year she was awarded a national research scholarship (from ESRC) to fund and successfully complete her PhD in Psychology at the same institution. Now a seasoned lecturer with specialism in the Psychology of Relating, Aneta is the Dean of School of Psychology at the University of East London (UK).

One

Introduction: Thrive at university

Christian van Nieuwerburgh and Paige Williams

Congratulations!

If you're reading this book, you've made it to university. This is a significant achievement! And, if you make the most of the opportunity, your time at university will prepare you for even greater achievements and accomplishments throughout your life. Of course, universities are respected centres of learning, but they are also exciting, vibrant social communities that can provide safe spaces for learning, for preparation, for striving and for experimentation. One thing we know for sure from our own experience – and perhaps even the *best* thing – is that you will learn so much more from your time at university than the subjects you are studying.

Why we wrote this book

We, the editors and chapter authors, are deeply committed to what universities stand for. We have all had the privilege of studying at university in many different parts of the world – from Australia and New Zealand to the USA, from the Middle East to Europe and the UK. Importantly, we all have experience of teaching in universities. Collectively, we have taught and supported tens of thousands of university students and we are passionate about the opportunities and choices that university education offers young people: it's what brought us together to write this book. In other words, we are passionate about your success! What sets us apart from many others who may wish you success is that we would like you to experience academic and professional success, while also growing personally and experiencing high levels of wellbeing. We don't see these things as being separate or mutually exclusive. We wholeheartedly believe that you, your friends, your programme peers and campus colleagues can learn to thrive during your years of university study. What does that mean? It means that you experience physical and psychological health, that you feel engaged, that you feel a sense of belonging and connection, and that you experience emotional wellbeing.

We are all positive psychology practitioners and academics, but we're not naïve. We are not suggesting that university is an easy ride. There will be ups and downs. Alongside moments of pure joy, there will be times of bitter disappointment. We are also not suggesting that you should just focus on the social aspects of university and party for three or four years (sorry, everyone!). Universities are a place of challenge – it *should* and will feel difficult at times. Being challenged and moving outside your comfort zone are both necessary if you are to grow into your potential. Alongside success, you may experience failure, disappointment, disengagement and even disillusionment with the choices you have made. This is all part of the journey – which is why we got together to produce this field guide.

Benefits to you

By reading this book, you will learn strategies, insights and hacks from some of the leading academics in the field of positive psychology. By using these strategies, you can get more out of your studies. Even better, you will learn ways of being successful as a student, while also enjoying the experience more. By feeling well and doing well at university, you are likely to make more friends and perform better in your examinations. All of this will lead to better outcomes at university which will lead to you having more choices when you graduate. Perhaps most importantly, the skills you develop as you read through this book and study at university will give you the confidence and knowledge to flourish in your life beyond education.

Outline of this book

Each of the chapters is written by an expert from the field of positive psychology. Positive psychology is the scientific study of optimal functioning. Its focus is on the positive aspects of being human, and its researchers study what is best about the human experience. Every chapter shares relevant insights from the field that may be helpful to you as you navigate your way successfully through your university years.

This chapter

This chapter sets the scene for the book, presenting you with an overview of what to expect. It's important for you to feel that *you* are making the choices in relation to your own success and wellbeing. By providing you with a brief outline of each chapter, you can decide what is most important to you. You may want to read the book in the order it is presented, or you may want to pick and choose which topics are most relevant to you at a given moment.

Chapter 2: Learn about how you learn

This chapter, written by us, the editors, provides some of the latest knowledge from neuroscience to shed light on how you can manage your brain most effectively for the purposes of learning. Understanding how you learn will have enormous advantages during your time at university. It will also have lifelong benefits.

Chapter 3: Identify your strengths

This chapter is written by Andrea Giraldez-Hayes, a leading academic within the fields of coaching and positive psychology, and with many years of experience of teaching at university. Andrea explains the importance of acknowledging and using your strengths while studying. The chapter will help you to become aware of your character strengths and to identify your core values in order to use these to thrive as a student.

Chapter 4: Be hopeful

This chapter is written by Rachel Colla, who is an award-winning university teaching specialist and executive coach who is passionate about supporting people to succeed. Rachel sets out the scientific evidence that supports the intentional use of hope as a way of achieving goals. The chapter will support you to access untapped energy and motivation by providing you with strategies to harness hope so that you can achieve your desired outcomes.

Chapter 5: Focus on what is possible

This chapter is written by Ana Paula Nacif, an executive coach, consultant and academic with expertise in group and team coaching and significant experience of working on wellbeing across a number of sectors. Based on research, Ana presents ways of increasing your chances of achieving goals that are important to you. The chapter sets out different types of goals and proposes practical strategies for goal-setting and attainment.

Chapter 6: Look after yourself

This chapter is written by Peggy Kern, a highly published academic on the topics of health and positive psychology, who is committed to bridging the gap between research and practice. Peggy is passionate about the importance of self-care. The chapter discusses how to manage stress and shows how you can integrate self-care into your university life through some practical and easily implementable strategies.

Chapter 7: Live in the moment

This chapter is written by Rona Hart, an expert in the psychology of change and an academic with an interest in empowering people and helping them to transform their lives. Rona will encourage you to be more mindful during your university years. The chapter starts with an overview of mindfulness before providing you with an understanding of how to practise it. The chapter includes some practical exercises which you can start doing immediately.

Chapter 8: Invest in relationships

This chapter is written by Aneta Tunariu, a well-respected academic and senior leader within the university sector, with expertise in the psychology of relating. Aneta is passionate about social justice and has designed interventions and programmes to support young people. This chapter considers why relationships matter and recommends ways to develop positive relationships during your time

at university. The chapter argues that positive relationships have multiple benefits: increased wellbeing, personal growth and the development of social capital.

Chapter 9: Prepare for adversity

This chapter is written by Hanna Kampman, a university lecturer who brings
together her interests in positive psychology, sports coaching and post-traumatic
growth. Through her personal and professional roles, she embodies many of
the principles of positive psychology. The chapter explores the best ways that
human beings can deal with adversity. It will provide you with insights and
practical ideas about how to develop the resilience you will need to successfully
complete your studies.

Chapter 10: Be playful

This chapter is written by Robert Biswas-Diener, a leading figure in the field of
positive psychology research and practice, with a specialist interest in happiness.
He is known fondly as the 'Indiana Jones of Positive Psychology' because of his
positive psychology research with groups such as the Amish, the Inuit and the
Maasai. The chapter proposes that being playful is an important aspect of leading a good life. The chapter also sets out the differences between adult and child
play and then highlights the benefits of play.

Chapter 11: Find meaning

This chapter is written by Michael Steger, a professor and an international authority on positive psychology, with a specialist interest in how 'meaning in life'
impacts wellbeing. Michael is a highly respected academic and researcher who
is committed to understanding how to foster wellbeing and reduce psychological
distress in people's lives. The chapter explores how the idea of 'meaning in life'
can have a deep impact on your life. The chapter will encourage you to reflect
on what is important in your life and to learn strategies to live in ways that align
with what is meaningful.

Chapter 12: Learn about yourself

This chapter is written by Aaron Jarden and Rebecca Jarden, a married couple
who are both passionate advocates of wellbeing. Aaron is a researcher, lecturer,
consultant and entrepreneur, while Rebecca is an academic and a lecturer in

nursing and critical care. Aaron and Rebecca will challenge you to take a more experimental approach to your lives. This chapter discusses the concept of 'positive failure' and gives you an opportunity to complete a self-assessment of your wellbeing.

Chapter 13: Care about the world

This chapter is written by Tim Lomas, a leading academic who has been at the cutting edge of research and theory in positive psychology. His research interests span mindfulness, Buddhism, linguistics and gender. In this chapter, Tim highlights the importance of *self-care* as a precondition for caring for others. The chapter suggests that caring for others has benefits for you, and proposes some practical ways to help you to be more caring during your time at university.

Chapter 14: Savour your experience

This chapter, written by us, the editors, provides a summary of what we have covered in the book. We review what we hope you have learned and share a few ideas about how you might use this information during your time at university and beyond.

Consistent structure

While you will have the benefit of the insights and expertise of a wide range of specialists, we have worked hard to ensure that there is consistency in the overall layout of the chapters. Each starts with an introduction and a clear outline of what you will learn. Then every chapter briefly surveys the research and theories relevant to the topic. This is because it is important that you know that there is evidence underlying the topic that is being presented. The main body of every chapter will be the practical implications for you. All the chapters conclude with some final thoughts and reflections from the authors.

Our intention

Our overriding intention is to be helpful to you by sharing what we know, rather than 'teaching' you about positive psychology. That is why each chapter provides a very brief overview of the research and theory relating to each topic before presenting some practical and actionable strategies that you may want to use. If you find it helpful, you can read through the entire book, enjoying each chapter in the order they are presented, or you can dip in and out of the book, selecting the topics that are of most interest to you at the time.

So, here's hoping that you're at the start of an enormously rich and fulfilling phase of your life. As the title of this book suggests, we would like you to thrive – and that means that we want you to *do* well and *feel* well during your time at university. We're encouraging you to enjoy it and get the most out of the experience. Above all, it is an opportunity for so much learning – about your subject, about yourself and about how you like to be with others.

Two

Learn about how you learn

Paige Williams and Christian van Nieuwerburgh

Learning about your brain

Everything you do, everything you feel, every experience you have is stored in your brain. It is the ultimate storage facility and central processing unit for your life. Understanding how the brain performs can help you learn better and create a more conducive context for this to take place (Blackwell et al., 2007; Dubinsky et al., 2019). Numerous studies have shown that raising the awareness of learners about how the brain develops can speed up learning and development (Halvorson et al., 2016). The bottom line is that your learning can be improved by you understanding how your brain works (Grah & Dimovski, 2014). Let's begin.

Your brain has one purpose in life

Contrary to popular belief, your brain's main job is not to *think*. No. Your brain's primary function is to effectively manage your 'body budget' so that you can *survive*, and hopefully also *thrive* (Barrett, 2017). The scientific name for this body budgeting process is *allostasis*, and it involves your brain predicting and preparing to meet the energy needs of your body before they arise so that you can take effective action as efficiently as possible to survive (Sterling, 2012; Sterling &

Laughlin, 2015). The 'gain' from this budgeting process is food, shelter, affection or physical protection so that you can play your part in nature's most vital task: continuing your genetic line.

And it's this most basic operating principle of the brain – the balance of 'pain' versus 'gain' for your body budget – that determines whether you do something or not. What we include under each of those words may be highly subjective and individual, but ultimately every choice we make is a call based on the pain-to-gain ratio for our body budget. Understanding the main purpose of the brain, what it prioritises and, in particular, how it learns, can help you be more effective in your learning. So let's take a look at how the brain learns.

How the brain learns

We are born with approximately 100 billion brain cells, or neurons. And while this number remains relatively stable, human brains are born 'under construction' and remain so throughout your life. By around the age of 25 years, your brain is at its full adult structure and function. However, what continues to grow and develop are the tens of thousands of connections that form between each one of these 100 billion neurons. These connections form neural pathways and networks, and their continual restructuring or change is known as *neuroplasticity*. It is through the process of neuroplasticity that your brain learns.

When you have new experiences or are exposed to new ideas, your brain creates new neural connections and pathways to accommodate the information. This is how your brain 'grows' – in density rather than size. Some of these pathways are used more frequently than others as you repeat particular actions or behaviours, or review and revise certain information. The connections between these neurons or within these neural networks build, becoming stronger and more developed, and, as a result, are more efficient transport routes for carrying and processing information. One of the founders of modern neuroscience, Donald Hebb, summarised this as 'Neurons that fire together, wire together' (Hebb, 1949). This became known as Hebb's Law and is a fundamental principle in how we learn. From a body budgeting perspective, your brain recognises this efficiency and so is more likely to use these stronger, more developed pathways and networks in the future. The opposite happens with neural pathways and networks that are used less often; they weaken, wither and are eventually trimmed. The saying 'use it or lose it' speaks directly to this process of building and trimming.

In this way, our brains develop neural networks that embed and store our learning. You have neural networks for every object, person, animal and situation you have ever encountered. The neural network for your perception of an apple will involve cells in different areas of your brain that code for the type, shape, feel, size, smell and taste of an apple, along with whether or not you like apples, when and where you last saw one, and ways to use them. It takes thousands of connected neurons in a neural network for 'apple' to create this representation each time you see, think about or just hear the word, 'apple'. And that's just an apple!

What does this mean for your learning?

The ideas, strategies and practices that we share with you in this book, and that you will engage with throughout your life at university, will have differing amounts of neural infrastructure in terms of the density of pathways and networks in your brain that support them. There may be some ideas that you've studied or come across before and that are able to be easily processed and understood because the neural networks are like a well-surfaced, six-lane highway that is easy, effective and efficient for the information to travel down. For new ideas, or those that you have had limited contact with before, the neural pathways and networks may not exist or may be undeveloped. This could be more like travelling down a bumpy, unsurfaced track in the wilderness as the learning, understanding and practice feel more effortful, take more energy and focus, and – to begin with at least – may not be as enjoyable.

Understanding that this is part of the learning experience can help you build these neural networks beyond unpaved tracks so that they are easier to traverse and experience. And while you may not choose to keep building every pathway and network into a six-lane highway, it's also important not to stop construction work too early or allow them to wither and be trimmed before you've given them a real chance.

Helping your brain learn: Your learning context

Learning doesn't happen in isolation; there are many influencing factors. Some of these are 'inside' you, such as the way you feel, your energy levels and your motivation. These things are also within your control. Other factors that impact learning are 'outside' us, both literally in terms of the physical environment, and also beyond our control, such as the way that other people feel and behave.

Here's an example of how 'inside' and 'outside' factors can influence our learning experiences. Imagine two individuals in two different learning contexts, where the goal in both is to learn to read braille. Both students come to the task with an equivalent cognitive ability and learning profile. Student A is provided with a complex manual, a passage in braille, seated in a cold classroom with no support, and no explanation for why they are learning braille. They are tired and feel anxious and fearful about how they will perform. Student B is provided with the same materials – the manual and passage – but they have an energetic and supportive teacher and are in a comfortable, familiar setting. Student B is well-rested, motivated and enthusiastic about being able to support their vision-impaired sister to learn to read after they have completed the task. Who do you think is more likely to master this task? When we look at it like this, it becomes obvious that the quality of learning outcomes is not just determined by an individual's cognitive ability; learning occurs in a broader context. This holistic understanding of learning recognises that the brain not only interacts with incoming information, but with the entire context in which it is presented. And this is why, to help our brain to learn, we must consider all the physical, cognitive, emotional and social factors within our learning context.

Physical factors

Many studies have highlighted the importance of nutrition in healthy physical and mental development. The brain draws approximately 20% of the body's available energy, and increased mental demands draw more oxygenated blood into the brain as neurons need fuel to fire. Dehydration and low glucose levels drain the body and the brain of their functional necessities and, in turn, inhibit the learning process.

Recent neuroscientific research points to the role of sleep in memory consolidation. Studies have shown that hippocampal neurons activated during learning tasks are reactivated during slow-wave sleep, reinforcing the neural network and consolidating the learning. In a study requiring participants to learn routes through unfamiliar streets, performance, as measured by error rates in the task, was significantly lower for those who had benefited from sleep. Other studies focusing on sleep loss provide clear evidence for lower academic performance caused by reductions in both declarative and procedural memory, suggesting that the prefrontal cortex is highly sensitive to sleep deprivation. What does this mean for you? Regular good quality sleep is a precursor for memory and learning.

Cognitive factors

Learning something new requires focused attention. To learn new information, it must be of interest, be meaningful and there should be limited distractions. This means no multi-tasking! Multi-tasking requires that you attend to more than one thing at a time. It *is* possible to multitask, and we're doing it all the time: cooking a meal while watching television, or taking down notes as you listen to a presentation. This impressive capability can be attributed to the basal ganglia in your brain – a complex set of subcortical structures that store your life experiences and create and maintain your daily conscious and subconscious habits. It's like the auto-pilot of your life.

Unfortunately, it is the prefrontal cortex, not the basal ganglia, that holds current information in working memory, consciously processes that information, and deals with new or complex issues. There is no autopilot here. And while the basal ganglia can draw on almost unlimited capacity, the prefrontal cortex has limited daily capacity and struggles constantly with what to prioritise and bring to conscious thought.

Studies have shown that performance deteriorates significantly as soon as we attempt more than one cognitively taxing task at a time. Each additional task you undertake concurrently with others reduces your performance on *all* tasks. Just try reading an article out loud while watching the news, or adding up a list of numbers while someone is speaking to you. This is because multitasking diffuses attention, compromises memory and reduces performance. Not only that, it's exhausting!

It can take up to 15 minutes to restore concentration following a distraction, due to what's called a 'refractory period' in the brain. Because of this, a temporary shift in attention from one task to another, for example when your phone 'pings', or someone stops for a chat and interrupts your work – increases the amount of time necessary to finish the primary task by as much as 25%. This phenomenon, known as 'switching time', drains our mental energy and makes it harder to get back to the task at hand. What does this mean for you? The brain is simply not designed for multitasking – minimise distractions to maximise learning uptake.

Emotional factors

Emotions are integral to thinking and learning. The amygdala, a small, almond-shaped part of our inner brain, is the seat of emotions and elicits the emotional response component of our behaviour. Amygdala activation during the encoding of a new memory enhances its subsequent retrieval.

This means that emotional cues linked to learning content forge a deeper and richer neural pathway than fact-based content alone. Further than amplifying memories and consequently learning, new research highlights that emotions are actually fundamental to cognition itself. Emotion regulates where we place our attention, and is essential to recruiting the neural networks on which we build our knowledge. In our earlier example of learning braille, emotion (the student's desire to assist their sister) generates the motivation to focus their attention on the task. In this way, emotion and thinking are integrally linked. What does this mean for you? Look for opportunities to generate positive emotions as you learn.

Social factors

Not much of our learning occurs in isolation. Throughout our childhood and adolescent years, we learn through direct experience or observation of others, as well as being taught in social establishments, such as school and college. Through these means, we not only create new learning, but we also test and validate our thinking. Learning communities reinforce learning outcomes, increase motivation and challenge, and generate more diverse solutions than individuals operating alone. The relationships we have in our learning contexts and environments – whether with teachers, peers or friends – play an important role in setting us up for learning success. What does this mean for you? Where possible, recruit learning buddies and create study groups – yes, even to support you to thrive and succeed!

Helping your brain learn: Your learning design

Learning context is important to learning outcomes. Some would say that the context is more important than cognitive capacity. But there is another leverage point that you have available to help your brain to learn, and that is how you design your learning experiences. The AGES model (Davachi et al., 2010) is a useful framework to use when considering this.

AGES is an acronym for Attention, Generation, Emotion and Spacing. Let's have a look at how each of these can be used in effective design to accelerate and maximise your learning.

Attention

Neural networks will be formed for everything to which we pay attention and nothing that we don't. Due to the vast amounts of information we encounter each day, we have evolved to selectively place our attention only on stimuli that are interesting or meaningful to us. Attention is the filter through which we see the world, and it accounts for why two people, observing the same situation, may have quite differing recollections of it: we literally see differently, based on what we attend to.

Attention requires focused concentration and is a prerequisite for neurons to be activated and neural networks to be forged. Forging new networks is energy-intensive and our brains are not designed to remain attentive for long periods of time. The brain needs down-time at regular intervals to rest and refocus. During this time, it is also strengthening the newly formed connections. When we push ourselves to focus beyond our natural limits, our concentration wanes, which is our brain's way of forcing a break – and we catch our minds wandering. What does this mean for you? Take regular brain-breaks and bring focused attention to learning opportunities.

Generative

The way that you learn now is very different than when you were a child. Children absorb everything about their world in an uncensored way and place total confidence in their caregivers – the adults around them. This is an important and necessary part of evolution as it allows 'cultural inheritance' – the passing on of cultural and social knowledge between generations – to take place without it being wired into our genes (Barrett, 2020). The same is not true for adults. We selectively choose what we learn based on what is relevant and of interest to us, building on prior learning and taking as much responsibility as we choose for our ongoing learning.

The adult brain has been described as a dynamic, plastic, experience-dependent, social and affective organ that is not just engaged in, but is driving, its own learning. Because of this, the more your brain is proactively involved in its learning, through the self-generation of ideas, strategies and actions, the more effective it becomes. As you choose where to begin with your journey to thriving, the critical words are 'relevance' and 'immediacy'. Research suggests that adults learn best by taking a problem-centered, rather than a subject-centered, approach, and so will you. What problems do you want to solve? What opportunity do you want to embrace? The key is that ownership of the process, as well as its outcomes, lies with the learner; and that's you. What does this mean for you? Be clear about what is most relevant to your thriving. Let that be what guides what you choose to learn.

Emotion

As we covered earlier when looking at your learning context, emotions bind memory. Like adding fuel to a flame, an emotional cue ignites more neuronal activity in more brain centres and, consequently, burns a deeper pathway. The vivid recollections we have of events in our life that carry rich emotional content are embedded through the activity of many thousands more neurons than is the case for 'normal' or unemotive events. And, while this applies to any 'flavour' of emotion, decades of research show that we learn better when we are in a happy, positive mood and when we are having fun. For example, studies show that including games in learning, with a relevant context, that require challenging technical skills and are appropriately debriefed on completion, add to the learning outcomes of all four of the Kolb learning styles – concrete experience, reflective observation, abstract conceptualisation and active experimentation. What does this mean for you? Consider how you can gamify your learning and make it playful and fun.

Spacing

A relatively simple way to leverage your outcomes through learning design is to intentionally consider how you 'space' out content. The limitations to your brain's prefrontal cortex capacity come into direct play when we are learning, as new information must take this route to be embedded as acquired skills and knowledge.

So, if you expect to begin at 8:30am and cram content back to back until 5:30pm, with only brief comfort and food breaks, you're actually breaking your biological limits and invariably, at the same time, limiting your learning uptake. The law of diminishing returns applies to learning due to our cognitive capacity. We need to respect our biology and work with, not against, its limitations.

What does this mean for you? Build in adequate time gaps for new learning to be digested, consolidated and rehearsed.

Summary

The brain is our central storage and processing facility for learning. To help it process and function as effectively as possible, there are a number of factors in our learning context and learning design that we can consider. These are:

- Physical context: regular good quality sleep is a precursor for memory and learning.
- Cognitive context: minimise distractions to maximise learning uptake.
- Emotional context: look for opportunities to generate positive emotions as you learn.
- Social context: recruit learning buddies and create study groups to support you to thrive and succeed.
- Learning design – attention: take regular brain-breaks and bring focused attention to learning opportunities.
- Learning design – generation: be clear about what is most relevant to your thriving and let that direct your learning.
- Learning design – emotion: make your learning playful and fun by gamifying it.
- Learning design – spacing: ensure that you have sufficient gaps in time for new learning to be digested, consolidated and practised.

Learning to thrive with the brain in mind

Your time at university is rich with the opportunity for learning – learning about your chosen field of study, about the people you study alongside, about life at university, about your friends and, most importantly, about yourself. The chapters that follow provide you with a variety of ideas to help you learn more about what supports your thriving, and tools and strategies so that you can experiment and learn what will work for you in your life, right now. The purpose of this chapter at this point in the book is that you understand how you can 'hack your brain' and go about this learning – and all the learning that you do – in the most effective way possible. We hope that it serves you well, in your learning-to-thrive journey, at university and beyond.

Three

Identify your strengths

Andrea Giraldez-Hayes

Introduction

If someone asked you who you *really* are, what your strengths are, or what is important to you, could you answer straight away? Many people would falter, and some might not be able to reply at all. However, trying to see yourself clearly and knowing your strengths and values are important for wellbeing and success in life. Not being aware of your strengths could hold you back from stretching yourself or may cause you to push yourself too far. Neglecting your values may lead to making choices that stir up inner conflict or decisions that do not serve you.

Research suggests that being aware of your strengths (Linley, 2008; Niemiec, 2018) and your values (Hayes et al., 1999; Schwartz, 2012) improves your understanding of yourself, your actions and your decisions. The question for us is: *how* do we get to know them? In addressing this question, this chapter invites you to discover your strengths and the values that drive your life, and to notice how they motivate you to do certain things and give meaning to your actions. By reading this chapter, and completing the suggested activities, you will achieve three learning goals:

- become aware of your character strengths
- identify your core values
- understand how to deploy your strengths and your values so that you can thrive.

Playing to your strengths

Have you heard the phrase 'play to your strengths'? You play to your strengths when you focus on your character strengths – positive characteristics such as kindness, hope or courage – and your performance strengths or talents – natural abilities such as perfect pitch or spatial reasoning. Although both are important, in this chapter we will focus on character strengths, defined as people's traits, reflected in their thoughts, feelings and behaviours that, when in balance, help them to flourish and thrive (Peterson & Seligman, 2004). Research suggests that using and developing strengths might lead to better outcomes than the traditional approach of overcoming weaknesses (Kauffman & Scoular, 2004; Peterson & Seligman, 2004). As a student, you probably remember your schooldays or conversations with your parents or caregivers when you were repeatedly told to work on your weaknesses or fix your failings. In comparison, your strengths might have been mentioned less frequently. These days, as an adult, you may have noticed how, in everyday conversations, people rarely talk about their strengths or find it hard to name them. In fact, it has been observed that only a third of people asked to list their strengths in surveys can do so (Hill, 2001, as cited in Linley & Harrington, 2006). The reasons can be twofold: that they do not know their strengths, and that they do not fully appreciate their value. However, studies show that recognising and using our character strengths have a positive impact on a wide range of outcomes, including wellbeing (Biswas-Diener et al., 2011; Wagner, 2020), health (Hausler et al., 2017), life satisfaction (Peterson et al., 2007) and resilience (Martínez-Martí & Ruch, 2017). Furthermore, spotting other people's strengths helps us to understand their positive traits and build better relationships with them (Green, 2019).

Values in Action (VIA)

Almost 20 years ago, Peterson and Seligman (2004) developed the VIA classification which identifies 24 character strengths organised around six virtues or 'core characteristics valued by moral philosophers and religious thinkers' (p. 13): *wisdom, courage, humanity, justice, temperance* and *transcendence*. These virtues are universal and cross-cultural, and the related character strengths contribute to their achievement. For example, the virtue of courage can be achieved by a combination of different strengths – *bravery, persistence, integrity* and *vitality* – although any given individual will rarely stand out in all of these strengths. According to Peterson and Seligman (2004), a person is of good character if they have a combination of one or two strengths in each group. We invite you to read the list of virtues and strengths presented in Table 3.1 and to consider what your top five character strengths might be.

Table 3.1 Virtues and character strengths

Wisdom	Courage	Humanity	Justice	Temperance	Transcendence
Curiosity	Bravery	Kindness	Teamwork	Forgiveness	Appreciation of beauty and excellence
Love of learning	Perseverance	Love	Fairness	Humility	
Judgement	Honesty	Social intelligence	Leadership	Prudence	Gratitude
Perspective	Zest			Self-regulation	Hope
Creativity					Humour
					Spirituality

Source: Adapted from Peterson & Seligman (2004)

Now that you are familiar with the list of virtues and character strengths, it might be helpful to discover your own five signature character strengths, as well as your middle and lesser strengths. Your signature strengths are those that come naturally and are essential to who you are when you are at your best. Generally, you use your signature strengths in all aspects of your life. That makes them different from your middle strengths, as these are situational or applied to specific domains. For example, they may come into play in your studies or when socially relating to others, but not all the time. Sometimes middle strengths can be used in combination with a signature strength. Let us suppose that love of learning is one of your signature strengths and curiosity one of your middle strengths. The latter may help you to keep asking questions or seeking new answers when you are trying to learn something new. Your lesser strengths will be the five at the bottom of your list. They are not weaknesses but strengths that do not activate as naturally as the others. Using them may require extra energy and effort. However, as with the middle strengths, you can deliberately develop them. For example, you can use your signature strength of kindness to increase your lesser strength of gratitude when you have the opportunity to give or receive gifts or help. If one of your lesser strengths is perseverance, you can decide to use it very intentionally when trying to achieve meaningful goals. One example would be to work out ways to persist when things get difficult.

Have you tried to identify your strengths? If so, that is a good beginning. However, there is another way to discover your strengths, namely taking the VIA Survey of Character Strengths. This is a self-report questionnaire. You can take it for free using this link: www.viacharacter.org.

Once you have discovered your strengths, you may want, as suggested by Seligman (2002, p. 151), to review your top five and, for each one, consider if each of these criteria applies:

- a sense of ownership and authenticity ('That is the real me')
- a feeling of excitement while displaying it, particularly at first
- a rapid learning curve as the strength is first practised

- continuous learning of new ways to enact the strength
- a sense of yearning to find ways to use it
- a feeling of inevitability using the strength ('Try to stop me')
- invigoration rather than exhaustion while using the strength
- the creation and pursuit of personal projects that revolve around it
- joy, zest and enthusiasm while using it.

According to Seligman (2002), if one or more of these criteria resonate with you while reflecting on one strength, you can be sure that this is a signature strength. Therefore, it would be a good idea to use such a strength deliberately in a variety of ways in many areas of your life, as explained below.

Using your character strengths

Using your signature strengths on a daily basis and in the main domains of your life will not only bring enjoyment and gratification but will also help you to flourish and thrive. That said, we need to add a note of caution. According to recent research (Niemiec, 2019), while optimal use of strengths is highly recommended, under- or overuse can have a negative impact. People usually underuse their lesser character strengths, however they can also underuse their chief ones. Let us imagine that one of your top strengths is perseverance: underuse might be giving up on your studies, work or other projects when you encounter problems. Knowing your strengths and being aware that it is possible to underuse them may help you decide consciously to deploy one or more strengths when appropriate. By contrast, in different circumstances, some people may tend to overuse one or more of their strengths. According to Niemiec (2019), 'when a strength is overused, it is having a negative impact on oneself or others so can no longer be considered a positive strength – it has become something else such as a negative habit or trait' (p. 456). For example, the overuse of perseverance may lead you to keep going even when you discover the project you are working on has lost its meaning. The overuse of love of learning may lead you to feel you never know enough and to keep trying to learn new things without taking enough time to consolidate what you already know.

Letting your values guide you

We can think of character strengths as the traits and resources we use to act in alignment with our values. One difference between values and virtues is that the first do not necessarily have a right or wrong meaning; they are right for you. So, when you think of your values, you think of what is important to you (e.g. freedom, pleasure, family, friends, work, success, altruism). Unlike strengths, the list of values is endless; you choose from a vast variety of options and they 'help you to place your feet in the right direction as you journey through life, no matter where life leads you' (David, 2018).

Everyone has a number of values with different degrees of importance attached to them (Schwartz, 2006), and just as with our character strengths, our values can be 'partly or wholly unconscious' (Vyskocilova et al., 2015). So, identifying your values and acting on them will help you to unlock your potential and live a more congruent and meaningful life. Knowing your values will prevent you from taking 'auto-pilot' decisions that might seem to be rational and inspired but end up not serving you well. For example, you might decide to work extra hours, including weekends, to make more money so that you can go out with your friends. If friendship is one of your core values but having money is not, you may end up having a values conflict when you discover that you have more money but no time for your friends!

Just as with character strengths, you can find different questionnaires online that may help you to identify and reflect on your core values – for example, the *Personal Values Assessment* (PVA) (www.valuescentre.com/tools-assessments/pva); the *Valued Living Questionnaire* (VLQ) (www.div12.org/wp-content/uploads/2015/06/Valued-Living-Questionnaire.pdf); or *Schwartz's Portrait Values Questionnaire* (PVQ) (https://discovermyprofile.com/tests). You can find out more about meaning and purpose in Chapter 11.

What theory and evidence show us: A summary

Up to this point, we have considered some theories and evidence related to the role that strengths play in our lives. As a summary, the main points to remember are:

- Being aware of your strengths gives you a better understanding of yourself, your behaviours and your decisions.
- Character strengths have been defined as people's traits reflected in their thoughts, feelings and behaviours that, when in balance, help them to flourish and thrive (Peterson & Seligman, 2004).
- Using and developing strengths might be more beneficial than the traditional approach of trying to identify and overcome weaknesses.
- Realising and using our character strengths has a positive impact on a wide range of outcomes, including wellbeing, health, life satisfaction and resilience.
- Spotting other people's strengths helps us to understand their positive traits so that we can build better relationships with them.
- Your signature strengths are those that come naturally and are essential to who you are when you are at your best.
- Using your signature strengths on a daily basis and in the main domains of your life will not only bring enjoyment and gratification but will also help you to flourish and thrive.

- Your values are the things that are important to you – the beliefs that motivate you and guide your decisions.

Putting theory into action

Up to this point, you have learnt about strengths and values, and you have probably realised that achieving a deeper understanding of yourself is fundamental to evolving as a person. Increasing your self-awareness helps you to recognise what you are naturally good at, what is important for you and which areas you may want to develop and change. All this knowledge is important, but it is not enough. In order to use your strengths and values to increase your wellbeing and to thrive, you need to put theory into action. In the same way that building your muscles requires exercise, so raising your self-awareness takes intentional exploration and practice of different ways of using your strengths and living a life aligned with your values. So, in this section we offer some suggestions for practice. Choose the ones that you find most compelling and invest some time in experimenting, reflecting and noticing what happens when you use your strengths and when you weigh up whether your decisions and actions are aligned to your values. If possible, write about your experience, reflecting on how you felt before, during and after each activity, and on how easy or challenging it was for you.

Understanding your strengths

If you have completed the VIA survey, you will already have discovered your strengths. Gaining a fuller understanding of them and how you use them in your everyday life are the natural next steps. You may want to start by reading the brief descriptions in Table 3.2 and thinking through the meaning of each strength.

Table 3.2 Virtues and character strengths with descriptions

Virtues	Character strengths	Description
Wisdom Cognitive strengths that require the use of knowledge	Curiosity	Having the desire to explore and discover; taking an interest in ongoing experience for its own sake
	Love of learning	Having a passion for learning, a desire to learn just for learning's sake
	Judgement	Making rational and logical choices, and analytically evaluating ideas, opinions and facts
	Perspective	Being able to 'see the forest as well as the trees', to avoid getting wrapped up in the small details when there are bigger issues to consider
	Creativity	Thinking of new ways to do things and produce original, useful and adaptable ideas or behaviours

Virtues	Character strengths	Description
Courage Emotional strengths that imply the determination to achieve goals, despite obstacles or difficulties	Bravery	Being able to face challenges, threats or difficulties - this involves valuing a goal or conviction and acting upon it, whether popular or not; it is facing - rather than avoiding - your fears
	Perseverance	Finishing things despite obstacles and sticking to your decisions - this includes perseverance and industriousness
	Honesty	Presenting yourself in a genuine and sincere way; taking responsibility for your feelings and actions
	Zest	Participating fully in life - this includes zest, enthusiasm, vigour and energy
Humanity Interpersonal strengths that involve supporting or protecting others	Kindness	Being compassionate, generous and nice to others
	Love	The degree to which you value close relationships with people and contribute to that closeness in a warm and genuine way
	Social intelligence	Being aware of yours' and others' motives and feelings
Justice Civic strengths that promote justice and healthy co-existence	Teamwork, citizenship and loyalty	Identifying with and having a sense of obligation to a common good - this includes social responsibility, loyalty and teamwork
	Fairness, equity and justice	Treating people justly; not letting your personal feelings bias your decisions about others
	Leadership	Having a tendency to organise and encourage a group to get things done, while maintaining good relations within the group
Temperance Strengths that prevent immoderation	Forgiveness and mercy	Being able to extend understanding towards those who have wronged or hurt us; to let go - forgiveness, and the related quality of mercy, involve accepting the shortcomings, flaws and imperfections of others and giving them a second (or third) chance
	Humility and modesty	Accurately evaluating your accomplishments
	Prudence	Being careful about your choices, stopping and thinking before acting
	Self-regulation	Controlling your appetites and emotions and regulating what you do
Transcendence Strengths that create connections with the wider universe and help to find meaning	Appreciation of beauty and excellence	Noticing and appreciating beauty, excellence and/or skilled performance in all domains of life, from nature and art to mathematics, science and everyday experience
	Gratitude	Feeling and expressing a deep sense of thankfulness in life, and more specifically, taking the time to genuinely express thankfulness to others

(Continued)

Table 3.2 (Continued)

Virtues	Character strengths	Description
	Hope	Having positive expectations about the future - this involves optimistic thinking and focusing on good things to come
	Humour	Recognising what is amusing in situations, and being able to offer the lighter side to others
	Spirituality	Includes meaning, purpose, life calling, beliefs about the universe, the expression of virtue/goodness, and practices that connect with the transcendent

Source: Descriptions adapted from VIA Institute on Character at www.viacharacter.org/character-strengths/appreciation-of-beauty-and-excellence

Once you have read the descriptions in Table 3.2, you may want to spend some time considering your five signature strengths and completing the following tasks:

- Recall a time when you were enjoying something you were doing and felt genuinely engaged and energised, a time when you were so focused on doing something that you lost track of time. What were you doing? What was happening around you? How were you feeling? Once you have called to mind a memorable event, consider which of your character strengths you were using.
- Recollect an occasion when you wanted to do something but let it go because you lacked the confidence or feared failure. Which character strength could have helped you to take action? How would that character strength have bolstered you?
- Consider how you are already using your character strengths in your studies, at work or in your personal life. Identify several clear examples.
- Now, imagine how you could use each one of your signature character strengths more often in your life, studies or work. For each strength, write a short action plan, outlining what you could do to boost it.

Using your strengths

Now that you understand your strengths and know about the benefits of using them, it is time to find opportunities to deploy them on a regular basis. The suggestion for practice is simple: choose one or two of your top strengths and decide on do-able actions you can undertake on a regular basis. For example, two of my strengths are appreciation of beauty and excellence, and curiosity.

I am lucky enough to live in London, with an enormous variety of architectural styles and curious nooks and crannies. I take different routes in my daily walks, making sure that I discover new places and enjoy the beauty of some of those buildings and locations.

Another option is 'using your strengths in new ways'. You just need to choose one of your top strengths, consider a new way of using it and do it for at least one week. Let us imagine that one of your chief strengths is perseverance. You may opt for one of the following:

1   Consider one task that you find meaningful and engaging but you have been putting off because you do not seem to have time for it. Create a plan to complete it in a reasonable period of time.
2   Set up one goal related to your health (for example, walk every day or eat five portions of fruit and vegetables a day) and stick to it for at least two months. A research study completed by health psychologists at University College London (Lally et al., 2010) suggests that, on average, it takes two months, more precisely 66 days, for a new behaviour to become automatic.
3   Grow a plant from a seed and keep tending it so that it grows and stays healthy.

What other options might you add to this list? Why not work out something similar for one of your own character strengths? If you need some more ideas, you can look over the many suggestions in *340 Ways to Use VIA Character Strengths* (Rashid & Anjum, 2011).

Developing your lesser strengths

Your lesser strengths also hold significant potential for growth. Compared to your signature strengths, using the lesser ones will require rather more effort and thought. However, it *is* worth trying. Simply choose the strength you would like to use and match it to a regular task or make a choice to use it on a one-off occasion. Let us suppose you choose kindness. You may decide to pick up groceries for a housebound neighbour when you do your own shopping. You could carry out a random act of kindness and, for example, send flowers or a gift to another student for no special reason. Whatever you choose, notice what happens to your mood.

Spotting other people's strengths

As you gain knowledge and understanding of your character strengths, you may also consider looking for strengths in others. While it is easy to spot weaknesses and imperfections in others, it is less common but highly beneficial to spot their strengths. How might you do that? Next time you meet your classmates or those people you study or work with, remind yourself to look for the best in them. What are they really good at? What is that character strength that makes them special? Once you have spotted one or two strengths, share what you have noticed by telling the person or sharing a note that includes an appreciation of their strengths. You could say, for example, 'from what you have said, I think one of your strengths is honesty'. If possible, follow up the conversation and let the other person agree (or disagree) and explain their reasons.

Considering your values

You may have taken one or all of the suggested questionnaires to identify your values. Now it is time to try some exercises to link them to practice.

- Think back to three 'peak moments' – three times that you can call to mind where everything seemed to be perfect and you felt fulfilled and engaged. Try to remember as much as you can and explore the details. Where were you? What was happening? Who was there? What made the experience so special and significant? What triggered those positive feelings? And, finally, what values were being honoured in this experience? Write your own list or choose one or more of the values you identified when completing the questionnaires.
- Now think back to three moments of deflation or despair, when everything seemed to be blocked and life felt frustrating. Where were you? What was happening? Who was there? What made the experience frustrating or discouraging? What triggered those negative feelings? And, finally, what values were *not* being honoured in this experience?
- Now we invite you to consider three of your values – three you feel are really essential. For each one, answer the following questions: (a) Why do you think this value is important to you? (b) When do you honour this value? Think of one or two specific examples; (c) How do you feel when this value is not being honoured by you or others? Identify one example and describe your thoughts, feelings and behaviour.
- Finally, it is highly recommended that you check how far you are living according to your values. Choose five of your top values and rate them using a scale of 1 to 10, with 1 being not living the value at all and 10 living it entirely. Now consider those rated below 7. What could you do to improve these scores? What one action could you take in the next few days to make sure that happens?

Final thoughts

Being a university student is a unique experience that can be fascinating but also challenging. As a student, you will recognise the opportunities to make new friends, get a good education that will allow you to pursue your ambitions, develop critical thinking and communication skills, or acquire practical experience by participating in clubs and activities. However, you will also face some challenges, such as adjusting to a new life and sometimes experiencing homesickness, making new friends, feeling the pressure of your workload or facing difficulties in managing your time effectively. Playing to your strengths will be helpful in dealing with both the opportunities and the challenges, and every time you are presented with one, you could ask yourself, 'what is the strength that might help me to make the most of this opportunity or overcome this challenge?' Something similar applies to your values. Are your experience and behaviour in conflict with your values? You may know that this is the case when you feel stuck, bored or overwhelmed. When that happens, you may want to ask yourself whether something is not aligned with one of your core values; if so, reconsider the situation and set an intention to recommit to your values.

Living out your strengths and values will help you flourish and give meaning to your life. Your time at university will give you many opportunities to learn about your strengths and understand your values better. Not only will you thrive, but those around you and the wider community will benefit, too. So, it really is worth taking the time to check and make sure you are using your strengths and honouring your values as much as possible.

Four

Be hopeful

Rachel Colla

Introduction

Be hopeful? You must be joking, right? Perhaps it might be a good time to take a look around the world right now! How on earth is being hopeful going to help? I wonder if you might humour me for a minute and think back to a time when you were genuinely hopeful about a goal that was really important to you. It might have even been hoping to get into university. As you think back to that experience, I invite you to think about how you felt, and what you did as a result of that hope. I ask our students this very question at the beginning of our courses to help bring to light the potential benefits that hope may provide. I often ask them to imagine they were describing this to someone who had never before experienced hope. In Figure 4.1, you'll see what hope is in their words.

Figure 4.1 Students describing hope

If you look carefully, you might notice words like perseverance, despair and loss. Our students have a very grounded experience of hope – it's certainly not all 'rose-tinted glasses'. In fact, when we ask students to tune into their own personal experience – not the scientific literature – they have a deep understanding of the power that hope can provide to support them in times of struggle, to propel them towards a future they desire, one that enables possibility.

This chapter is designed to reinforce that experience by outlining some of the scientific evidence behind this, together with strategies to build hope to better enable your capacity to thrive at university and beyond.

Upon completion of this chapter, you will be able to:

- discover the impact that hope can have in supporting your goal achievement
- recognise the untapped energy that hope can provide to fuel your motivation, persistence and wellbeing
- identify strategies that can build your creative and divergent thinking
- design a map that leverages the power of hope towards your key goals.

Hope: The evidence

Unfortunately, hope is often misunderstood. There is a perception that hope is just wishful thinking or 'blind optimism' that things will turn out OK. Let's be clear, hope is not a spectator sport! In fact, a significant body of evidence demonstrates that hope is far more action-oriented than you may first think. It is linked to specific goals we want to achieve – not just a generalised belief in a positive future. This generalised belief is more reflective of optimism – a related, but distinct, construct (Gallagher & Lopez, 2009).

Before we go any further, let's take a moment to clarify the difference between the two. While both optimism and hope include positive future expectations, optimism does not necessarily reflect a belief in our ability to create that future, and thus some have suggested that optimism may be more relevant in areas where we have little personal control (Gallagher & Lopez, 2009). Compared with optimism, hope is more focused on what we can do or the *self-initiated actions* we can take to achieve our goals (Alarcon et al., 2013). The evidence to date shows that hope is a strong source of resilience and positive adaptation in most circumstances, with little evidence that you can have 'too much' hope (Snyder, Rand et al., 2002).

What is hope theory?

While there are different conceptualisations of hope across a variety of disciplines, it is Rick Snyder and colleagues' (Snyder, Harris et al., 1991) theory that has dominated the scientific study of hope over the last 40 years. Hope theory is based on the understanding that the pursuit of goals is a key organising principle of human behaviour. Hope is reflected in our thinking around how we can best follow these pursuits (Snyder, 2002). As such, hope is a dynamic motivational state that comes from a belief in our *ability* to reach our desired goals (willpower), together with *planning* to meet those goals (waypower) (Snyder, Irving et al., 1991). We can summarise hope as:

$$Hope = Willpower + Waypower$$

Hope: The will and the way

The willpower element of hope is fuelled by a sense that we can make progress towards our goals and persist in the face of obstacles. Evidence suggests that rather than becoming discouraged when faced with obstacles, individuals with high levels of hope are more likely to lean into them with increased willpower that re-energises their persistence (Snyder, Rand et al., 2002). But willpower alone is not enough. A person can be highly motivated to move towards their goals, without clear strategies to achieve them (this is often what people call to mind when they think of hope), and this is where waypower comes into the hope equation. Waypower is fuelled by pathway thinking that allows us to come up with a variety of ways to achieve our goal. It encompasses divergent and creative thinking that broadens our perspective on the possibilities available, and enables us to tap into the resources required to support our goal achievement. This is critical in terms of overcoming the obstacles that will often show up as we work towards our goals. When willpower and waypower combine, they create a sense of goal-directed energy that supports fast and fluid thinking, which in turn enhances coping and our ability to adapt, change and grow (Snyder, 2002).

What are the benefits?

In general, individuals with high levels of hope are energetic and intrinsically motivated; able to set clear goals that are based on their own standards rather than on those of other people; and perceive obstacles as challenges that they can overcome with contingency planning (Chang, 1998; Gallagher et al., 2017; Lopez, 2013; Snyder, 2002). A range of studies have also demonstrated that hope is a key protective and enabling factor for a range of positive outcomes that are of interest, including:

- academic performance (Marques et al., 2017)
- retention at university (Gallagher et al., 2017)
- goal attainment in a variety of performance domains (Feldman et al., 2009)
- buffering against difficult experiences in life (Valle et al., 2006)
- high feelings of self-worth and low levels of depression (Snyder et al., 1997).

The evidence suggests that the effect of these benefits extends beyond university and into the workplace as well. For example, the results of a meta-analytic study demonstrated that high levels of hope led to a range of positive outcomes, including increased workplace performance, job satisfaction, work commitment and wellbeing (Reichard et al., 2013). So, if you develop your hope-building skills now, you'll feel the positive payoff for many years to come!

One explanation for the relationship between hope and the many positive outcomes described above can be understood through the value of hope as a resource (Conservation of Resources Theory (COR); Hobfoll, 1998). According to COR, the presence of adequate personal resources – such as skills, social networks and free time – contributes to our wellbeing. Hope is a psychological resource in and of itself, but it can also facilitate the acquisition of other resources (Hobfoll, 2002). In essence, hope broadens our thinking, allowing us to tap into both internal and external resources that can help in fuelling our persistence and mitigate some of the transitional challenges of moving into and out of university.

One of the concerns of psychological resources like hope is that it is finite and can become depleted when situational demands are excessive. However, emerging evidence suggests that this may not be the case for hope. For example, a study that examined seven adaptability factors to determine what predicts resilience in university students found that hope was the only characteristic (ahead of use of strengths, grit and control of one's beliefs) that prospectively predicted resilience, especially in response to uncertainty (Goodman et al., 2017). This makes hope a critical construct to consider as we prepare for a volatile, uncertain, complex and ambiguous world.

A summary of the evidence

- Hope is more than just wishful thinking. It is the combination of a belief in our ability to work towards our goals (willpower), together with the planning to reach those goals (waypower). This creates a sense of goal-directed energy that fuels our persistence, even in the face of obstacles.

- Students who have high levels of hope experience a range of positive university-related outcomes, such as increased motivation and wellbeing, and better academic performance, and are better equipped to set goals based on their own standards.
- Hope can be considered a resource in and of itself, but it is also helpful in acquiring other resources that enable us to thrive.
- Hope is also a key protective factor in the face of uncertainty and challenge. It is particularly useful as we transition into and out of university.

Putting it into action: Building willpower and waypower

While some of us will have 'naturally' higher levels of hope than others, a personality trait that was developed throughout our early life experiences, the evidence demonstrates that hope is something we can develop, even into adulthood (Feldman & Dreher, 2012; Pedrotti et al., 2008; Weis & Speridakos, 2011). We also know that hope can exist as a momentary experience (Martin-Krumm et al., 2015), and that hopeful thinking can be specific to an area of life, such as education, sport or work (Magyar-Moe & Lopez, 2015; Snyder, Feldman et al., 2002). This section will outline some key practices you can implement to be hopeful by developing:

- willpower: building your 'motivation muscles' to move into action
- waypower: developing your divergent and creative pathway thinking to design your way forward.

You might like to think about these practices as laying the foundation for hope to be ignited. The final activity in this section ignites that fuel by leveraging the iterative power of these elements. We use the term 'practices' very intentionally here, to demonstrate that these are not a 'one-shot effort'; but rather, through the intentional cultivation of hope practices, we can move from momentary experiences to increasing hopefulness as an enduring part of our resource kit.

Willpower (Agency)

Traditional goal setting relies on clarity in the specifics that we are trying to accomplish (see Chapter 5) and the willpower to achieve them. While we can rely solely on willpower to achieve our goals, these efforts at self-control can become exhausting and ignore the psychological force that we activate when we tap into hope.

One of the unique characteristics of us as a human race is our capacity for prospection – the ability to imagine, in detail, a variety of possible futures (Seligman, 2018). In fact, agency thinking may best be conceptualised as imagining the future, running multiple simulations and then deciding among them (Seligman, 2018). This creates a sense of motivating energy that pulls us forward – and it is this motivation that we will explore in the following practice.

Future-casting: Building a hope mood board

Shane Lopez, one of the leading scholars in hope theory, had a unique talent for articulating how this could be translated into practice, particularly in education settings. He coined the term *future-casting* to encompass this prospection aspect of hope (Lopez, 2013). Future-casting is the practice of imaging ourselves forward into the future to develop our agency thinking. Doing so taps into the relationship between hope and optimism that can support our motivational energy, because when we see a direct connection between the future we want and our behaviours and attitudes today, effort and commitment soar. The following practice is an adaptation of Laura King's (2001) 'Best Possible Self' activity, that has a significant evidence base to support its use in activating optimism (Carrillo et al., 2019):

1   Find a quiet place and time, where you can set aside around 15 minutes of quiet reflection. This is an investment in you and your future, so create the environment accordingly.

2   Using the prompt below, close your eyes and image yourself into the future for around 5 minutes.

> *Imagine yourself in the future, you can choose how far – 1 year, 5 years, 10 years … It doesn't matter as long as you project yourself into a day where you feel fully energised, where you are thriving. You have worked hard and succeeded at accomplishing your life goals. Think of this as the realisation of your life dreams, and of your potential. You are identifying the best possible way that things may turn out in your life, in order to help guide your decisions now.*

3   Try to bring this to life in as great a detail as possible: What are you doing? Where are you? Who are you with? How do you feel? Use all your senses. When thoughts pop into your mind about the obstacles that might impede the realisation of this vision, just acknowledge that there will be time for you to address these concerns, and gently return to imagining what is possible.

4   Spend the next 10 minutes capturing these details in a journal. You can choose what format works best for you to convey the essence of what you imagined: free flow writing, drawing, mind-mapping. The format doesn't

matter, but it is important to keep going for 10 minutes. This allows you to move beyond the immediately obvious to some of the deeper details that you imagine. These details may seem irrelevant now, but can form a significant part of your design going forward.

5   The final step is to create a personalised mood board that represents the essence of this imagined future. While there has been prolific use of vision boards to support motivation, these tend to focus on very specific outcomes that can be constraining. Instead, you are encouraged to build a visual organisation of ideas that inspire hope. Try to focus more on 'how' or 'why' this inspires you, rather than the 'what', as this can enable you to unlock a variety of different pathways towards that imagined future.

Waypower (Pathways)

As the title suggests, it is time to unlock the powerful combination of pathway thinking that can enable hope to emerge as we plan how to bring this to fruition. One of the downsides of traditional 'reverse engineering' or 'backwards mapping' approaches to goal planning is that it is predicated on a belief that there is one right way to achieve the goal. However, developing our capacity for divergent thinking can enable unexpected connections between ideas, thus facilitating a more novel approach to problem solving (Grant, 2016). Divergent thinking is effectively an executive function that is founded on managing interference from several sources, to allow a broader range of pathways to be developed (Nusbaum & Silvia, 2011). While divergent thinking is often thought of as being synonymous with creative thinking, it is actually just one part of the creative process. It has been associated with problem solving, ideation and creative potential (Nusbaum & Silvia, 2011; Runco & Acar, 2012). It is also an important precursor to pathway thinking that contributes to a sense of hope.

─────────────────────── ACTIVITY ───────────────────────

Preparing to plan

While many of our current practices encourage contingent (e.g. 'If this happens, then I will...') or convergent (analysing/evaluating the options) decision-making processes, our challenge here is to remain open to many possibilities. You may like to engage in the following primer practice before embarking on your own pathway planning to build your divergent thinking:

(Continued)

- Take 3 minutes to come up with as many uses as you can think of for a paper clip. You may experience a 'lull' in idea generation but push past this to make the most of the full 3 minutes.
- Reflect on what strategies you utilised to push past the lull and how you managed interference from obvious uses, or any feelings you may have experienced as ideas seem to dry up.

I wonder how you would find the primer practice if you completed it in a group? Do you think you would come up with the same volume and/or quality of ideas? Having completed this activity with thousands of participants, I can tell you that those that ideate in groups consistently produce a greater number of ideas. Of course, idea volume is not necessarily an indicator of greater quality. However, it does help us see connections and differences between ideas and therefore supports novel problem solving. When we ideate in groups, we are leveraging the power of synergy and different perspectives that provide sparks to ignite our own imagination.

There is a growing body of evidence that calls for a more socially connected view of hope. For example, Lee and Gallagher (2018) note that individuals with high levels of hope actively seek the support of others in working towards their goals, but are also likely to support the goal pursuits of others, serving to strengthen social bonds. This next practice is designed to reflect that, looking at how you can tap into the wisdom of your social connections to build hope.

Building a ColLab

There are many names for groups that create collaboration and community: wisdom circles, mastermind groups, personal board of directors. One that best represents the intention to build hope is ColLab, representing the importance of collaboration but equally the laboratory or experimental nature of the interactions that will support the development of pathway thinking:

1   In building your ColLab, you intentionally want to include people who think differently to you to help spark that divergent thinking and creativity, but who may share similar aspirations or values. Make two lists of people you know (remember, these don't only need to be your close contacts): one list that includes those who think differently from you and one that includes those who share similar values. Feel free to dream big about who is on this list. You don't have to actually invite them but this can help in identifying thinking or values that are important to you!

2   Shortlist down to those who would make both lists, or you may select key people from each list to invite to your ColLab to ensure a strong balance.

3   You might like to run a trial session of this ColLab by inviting them to help you brainstorm specific pathways to a chosen goal that is not high stakes for you. This gives you an opportunity to check-for-fit, as well as check-for-process, testing out what ground rules might need to be set up to maximise the opportunity for hope to emerge, not just for you but also for your collaborators.

Designing a hope story map

So, now you have strategies to build the willpower and waypower elements of hope! It is important to remember that hope is a *dynamic* motivation system and it is the *interactions* between these elements that empower hope to emerge. This final activity will help you to unlock the full power of hope as you design a map towards a goal that is meaningful for you. This strategy is built on the demonstrated efficacy of both cognitive and narrative approaches to building hope (Cheavens et al., 2006; Hedtke, 2014; Lopez et al., 2000). It is a fusion of Shane Lopez's hope mapping technique, together with Joseph Campbell's story archetype, the Hero's Journey, that has been shown to be an effective mapping process for change (Williams, 2019). In this practice, you will create a storyboard using the prompts below. There is no right or wrong way to map this out. The guides below will help you find your way. Figure 4.2 is your compass to guide you through the process. You can follow the arrow direction, but you might notice that there are also 'spokes' that allow you to double back if you need! Remember that all the way through this process you are drawing on the interconnections and energy of hope.

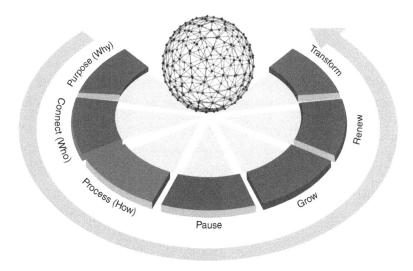

Figure 4.2   Your compass to hope

Before embarking on any epic journey, we need to consider what we will pack. In this instance, you need to 'go light but impactful'. Therefore, we invite you to consider what strengths and values (see Chapter 3) you have that might guide you on your journey. Make a list of these before you begin.

Why?

When we set goals that are aligned to our sense of values and purpose, we have the opportunity to supercharge our willpower. This sense of purpose, or whypower, can serve as a self-organising principle that guides decisions about our finite resources, as well as providing energy and motivation that lead to greater persistence (Mascaro & Rosen, 2005; McKnight & Kashdan, 2009). In this first step, reflect on your intention for this journey. Beginning with this in mind, rather than a specific outcome, can enable greater flexibility in the pathways you design. Note down a hope goal that moves you towards authentic purpose, which Keyes (2011) defines as 'a quality of being determined to do or achieve an end ... that employs one's gifts, brings a deep sense of worth or value, and provides a significant contribution to the common good' (p. 286). This is your call to adventure!

Who?

It's now time to choose a mentor to guide you on your journey. Whose wisdom could you tap into? Who may have travelled a similar road or who inspires a sense of hope in you? Note down the questions you have for them.

How?

This is where your story really gets interesting – it's time to 'choose your own adventure'! Map out a minimum of three different storylines that could move you towards your intention. This could be done alongside your mentor or may be inspired by others who have journeyed before you. There are no limits here to your creativity in how this story might unfold.

Grounding

Of course, in any good story there are obstacles to be faced, things that ground us on our epic journey. This is where we take a grounded approach to hope, not blind optimism. For each of your storylines, write in the obstacles or 'dragons' your hero may encounter.

Growth

In order to move the story forward, we need to consider the skills or resources that will help us overcome the 'dragons'. Sometimes this might mean pruning things that we have been hanging onto in order to grow into this challenge. Make a note of your growth opportunities and some emerging ideas of how this may change your story.

Renewal

At this point in the story, the hero can often feel tired or disappointed as they experience major setbacks. There are times when it is important to pause on the journey, to refuel, to take stock, before facing the final 'supreme ordeal' on the road to our goal. Consider here what renews your energy and write in your storyline your strategy to refuel. This could be the return of your mentor or time alone to reflect.

Transformation

In the final chapter of your journey, the hero reaches their goal, but they may arrive at a different end point than originally thought. What is common to all great stories is that they arrive with a new awareness that the impossible may now be possible, and that they have been transformed through the journey. You may not yet be able to write this part of your storyboard but you may reflect on how you might be transformed, inspired by the symbol of the dragonfly. In almost every part of the world, the dragonfly symbolises change, transformation, adaptability and self-realisation. This transformation often has its source in the mental and emotional maturing that is gained through the journey. The dragon-fly has been a symbol of hope, happiness, new beginnings and change for many centuries.

Final thoughts

The story does not end here, as we know that all good stories are just the seed for the next epic adventure. We know that the transition from secondary school to university can create significant levels of stress (Pritchard et al., 2007), but a sense of hope has been shown to be a key protective factor in this demanding academic system (Davidson et al., 2012). By investing in building hope in your life, you have the opportunity to build a resource system to support you to thrive while at university – and you can also play a role in igniting hope for others. For further support on that journey, you may like to check out www.hopelabs. com.au/storiesofhope.

This world needs your stories of hope. Imagine how the world could be different if we were to build a community of hope-filled leaders who catalyse a ripple of hope across the globe. That ripple can begin with you, today.

Five

Focus on what is possible

Ana Paula Nacif

Introduction

Human beings are born to thrive. We yearn for whatever we believe will enhance our lives. Some of the things we yearn for are more elusive than others, but that does not stop us from trying. How do we set out to achieve what we want for ourselves? This question brings two things to mind: choices and dreams. In relation to the first, I believe in a person's right to choose what is truly meaningful to them. In relation to the latter, the saying 'a dream without a goal is a wish. A goal without a plan is just a dream' (unknown) reinforces the idea that *wanting something* is not always sufficient.

Humans are unique in the way we think about ourselves in relation to time – past, present and future. We consider what we desire and want, now and in the future, and we are able to make plans and take action towards fulfilling our ambitions and aspirations. Having goals gives us the ability to steer our lives in the direction of our choice, giving us more sense of control over our path. It also helps us understand our thoughts, feelings and actions.

This chapter will share with you some of the theories about goal setting and goal attainment, as well as research findings, in this area. In this chapter, you will:

- learn about different types of goals
- understand the factors that can support you to achieve your goals
- explore different perspectives on goal setting and attainment
- learn strategies to consider your own goals and get motivated.

Where it all begins

The inspiring quote, 'a journey of a thousand miles begins with a single step', which is attributed to the Chinese philosopher Lao-Tzu, reminds us that to achieve something we need to take that crucial first step. Strictly speaking, the journey begins before that; it starts with knowing or considering the destination. To get somewhere, you need to decide *where* you are going – in other words, your goals.

Ordinarily, a goal can be defined as an aim or a desired result, but scholars have explained goals in many different ways. Little (1989) explored the concept of personal projects, which included actions ranging from 'the trivial pursuits of a typical Tuesday' (e.g. 'cleaning up my room') to the magnificent obsessions of a lifetime (e.g. 'liberate my people'). Emmons (1992) talked about people who set goals in 'primarily broad, abstract, and expansive ways', called high-level strivers, while others frame their goals in more concrete, specific, superficial terms, called low-level strivers.

It is clear, therefore, that not all goals are equal. Some researchers put goals in three categories: behavioural, performance and learning (Latham et al., 2016). A performance goal is focused more on the outcome than on the behaviours needed to achieve that outcome. For example, getting the highest marks in a chemistry assignment is a performance goal. Fully concentrating during chemistry lessons by banning external distractions is a behavioural goal. Gaining a deep understanding of the concepts covered in class would be a learning goal. Why do these categories matter? They matter because your goal will focus your attention (outcome, doing or learning). It will also have an impact on how you feel and your levels of motivation.

Goals are part of our everyday lives. We tend to set them using three categories:

1   Level of specificity: from very specific (i.e. eat five portions of fruit and vegetables every day) to more generic (i.e. have a healthy lifestyle).
2   Timing: short term (i.e. run 30 minutes today) to medium to long term (i.e. run a marathon next year). In this example, we can see that both are important, with the short-term goal supporting the long-term one.
3   Towards versus away from: to be healthy versus to avoid illness.

We are likely to use these categories to set goals in different areas of our lives. For example, we might be more specific in some areas (e.g. 'go to the gym three times a week') than others ('have a fun social life'), or seek to avoid ('manage my monthly budget so that I don't get into debt') or move towards something ('find a summer job to save money for a holiday'). The various categories of goal can support your wants and needs and help you to make choices on a day-to-day basis.

There is one crucial criterion that enables us to achieve most goals: sustained effort. We have all been in situations where, regardless of a bucket load of good intentions, we start working towards something before losing momentum, interest and energy. Unsurprisingly, research shows that it is much easier for us to keep going when we feel excited and inspired by our goals. Intentional change theory (Boyatzis & Howard, 2013) explains that when we identify a desired vision or purpose, we are able to convert it into a learning agenda. Now you know why goals that fit into the 'ought to' category are not always inspiring and may require extra effort to be achieved.

From aspiration to reality

Now that you know that identifying a desired vision makes it more likely to sustain effort, the next question is 'what else can help in setting and achieving your goals?' Goal setting theory (Locke & Latham, 2002), which is based on decades of research and field studies, tells us that people are more likely to achieve harder, more specific goals than easier, non-specific ones. This is because more challenging goals demand more energy to be achieved, requiring us to put more effort into achieving them. Other crucial factors are being committed to the goal, having the ability to achieve it and getting feedback on progress: 'So long as a person is committed to the goal, has the requisite ability to attain it, and does not have conflicting goals, there is a positive, linear relationship between goal difficulty and task performance' (Locke & Latham, 2006, p. 265).

Your belief in your abilities is incredibly important. Henry Ford's famous quote 'Whether you think you can, or you think you can't – you're right' illustrates the point that your beliefs will guide your actions and impact the outcomes. This personal judgement about your skills in any given circumstance is called self-efficacy. According to self-efficacy theory (Bandura, 1997), the more we believe we can do something, the more we commit to taking the required actions towards achieving it and, as a result, our goals are more likely to be achieved. For example, if you believe you can achieve good grades in a particular essay, you become more motivated to do what is necessary to do well: 'Unless people believe they can be successful in obtaining desired outcomes, they have little incentive to undertake activities or to persevere in the case of difficulties or failures' (Caprara et al., 2006, p. 32).

Growth versus fixed mindset

The way you think about goals is linked to your mindset, which is how you perceive the world. You may have already come across the concept of growth and fixed mindsets. Research shows that individuals who believe their talents can be developed (through hard work, good strategies and input from others) have a growth mindset (Dweck, 2017). These people tend to achieve more than those with fixed mindsets, who believe that their talents are innate and they cannot develop new ones. For example, consider the difference between 'I'm not good at maths yet' (I will continue to work at it to expand my knowledge) and 'I'm not good at maths' (it doesn't matter how much effort I put into it, I will never be able to learn maths). What happens as a result is a self-fulfilling prophecy. If you believe you can learn maths, you put effort into it and improve. If you think you will never be good at maths, you don't put effort into it; therefore you don't improve, confirming your initial view. According to researcher Carol Dweck, who coined the term 'growth mindset', a *pure* growth mindset doesn't exist. Instead, we all have a mixture of fixed and growth mindsets, which we develop and change throughout our lives.

More likely than not, your own goals are likely to be guided by your mindset. You may notice that you put more effort into the things you believe you can improve, while settling for less in other areas. The questions to ask yourself are:

- Are you shortchanging yourself?
- What would happen if you dared to add the little word 'yet' to the things you feel might not be possible?
- When you consider your goals and plans, what is one thing you can do *right now* to make progress?

The power of 'baby steps'

One way to boost your sense of self-efficacy is to make sure you build some wins into your journey towards your goals. Goal theory suggests that if a goal is too big or too complex, it should be broken down into smaller chunks to increase the likelihood of the person achieving it. In other words, if you want to climb Mount Everest, you may want to identify various sub-goals, such as: build your fitness levels, save money for the trip, and increase your mental toughness. Furthermore, each of these sub-goals can be broken down further and have their own plan and actions.

When it comes to actions, research shows that focusing on smaller micro-actions can lead to macrochanges in the long run. A study of 28 undergraduate students from the University of Kentucky showed that several microactions brought about positive macrochanges in participants' lives, including improved academic performance (Kim, 2014). Among these microactions were waking up 10–20 minutes earlier in the morning; putting the phone away during class; writing down plans in assignment planners; briefly reviewing course material;

and exercising. The key here is that these microactions require little time, effort and resources, and, therefore, can be undertaken on a regular basis.

So, if you are struggling with the bigger actions you would like to take towards your goals, think about microactions that you could commit to today. For example, it is much easier to commit to reading one book chapter than to studying for five hours. The thing about microactions is that, because they are achievable, you are more likely to complete them. Success in completing the microactions will support your sense of achievement and self-efficacy, which will motivate you to do more. Research shows that people feel positive emotions when they achieve their goals or make progress towards them (Snyder, Shorey et al., 2002). So, the end result is that you will feel good about yourself and inspired to continue pursuing your goals. Microactions are your friends; make sure to include them in your day-to-day life to boost your confidence and sense of wellbeing.

Energy to keep going

What do you need to propel you into action? Well, the answer is down to you as an individual. Some scholars have posited that there are three basic psychological needs that motivate us. These are autonomy, competence and relatedness, which are also the psychological needs that support people's wellbeing (self-determination theory; Ryan and Deci, 2001). Autonomy is about knowing that we have the freedom to make our own choices; competence is related to the belief that we can do something well; and relatedness is about feeling connected to others.

Self-determination theory is interested in what drives people to choose their goals – either towards intrinsic or extrinsic needs. Extrinsic motivation is associated with external rewards such as status, money and praise, whereas intrinsic motivation comes from personal satisfaction or growth. Studies have found that intrinsic goals tend to be linked to higher levels of wellbeing, more autonomy and improved performance. In addition, 'pursuing goals with strongly salient extrinsic content (e.g. wealth, image, and fame) tends to be associated with poorer mental health than does pursuing goals with strongly salient intrinsic content (e.g. relationships, growth, community, and health)' (Vansteenkiste et al., 2004, p. 246). You will probably be motivated by both intrinsic and extrinsic needs across all the different types of goals you set in your life, and it is important to remind yourself that those driven by intrinsic needs may hold the key to a more fulfilling life.

Making your heart sing

Furthermore, you are more likely to stick to intrinsically motivated goals. Research shows that people who choose self-concordant goals – those which are aligned to their interests and values – are more likely to achieve them and to experience increased wellbeing (Burke & Linley, 2007). In a series of three studies, researchers Sheldon and Elliot (1999) showed that individuals make more progress towards self-concordant goals and that the attainment of self-concordant goals leads to enhanced wellbeing. This is because individuals are more likely to put sustained effort into achieving self-concordant goals. Besides, when their targets are achieved, individuals feel 'experiences of autonomy, competence, and relatedness that are essential to enhanced well-being' (Sheldon & Elliot, 1999, p. 485).

This thinking is also supported by intentional change theory, which sets out the notion that goal setting works best when aligned to what matters most to the individual. It goes on to explain: 'when intentional change begins by connecting to the Ideal Self [who I want to be], the change process becomes grounded in intrinsic motivation, personal passion, resonant meaning, and belief in possibility' (Boyatzis & Howard, 2013, p. 215). The authors explain that the sustained change is moved by vision, which drives change by providing focus and energising the person both psychologically and physiologically (p. 218).

Taking the lead

It is an amazing feeling when you are able to align your goals and aspirations to your values. However, sometimes you may feel that you have no choice. This feeling can be disempowering and lower your motivation to pursue the things you want for yourself.

In psychology, researchers study what they call 'locus of control', which refers to people's generalised perception of control (Daniels & Guppy, 1997). Whereas self-efficacy relates to one's belief that one can succeed at something, locus of control is about how much control people feel that they have over particular situations. Those with an internal locus of control view themselves as the primary determinants of what happens to them, and those with an external locus of control see external factors, such as chance and powerful others, as the primary determinants of what happens to them (Rotter, 1966).

As you might expect, the degree to which you feel you have control of your circumstances will have a direct impact on how you feel about your personal goals and choices. It is always worth reflecting on your views around personal choice and what is within your sphere of influence. You cannot control everything, but you still have a choice of how to interact with these situations. For example, if you play basketball and you get injured just before the final few matches, there is very little you can do to change the fact that you will not be playing in the finals. However, how you deal with that situation and what you choose to do instead are entirely up to you. You may decide to stay in your room for a month, feeling sad about the situation, or you may decide to use the downtime for something that you kept putting off for lack of time, or you may decide to attend the training and the games to support your team. Each of these choices will have a distinct impact on how you feel and some will be more positive than others.

Theory and research around goals is a fascinating and growing area of knowledge. Although no one size will fit all, here are some key points worth considering when setting your own goals:

- Having goals gives us a sense of direction and choice. Remember that not choosing is also a choice!
- Goals can be specific or more generic; short or long term; towards or avoiding something.
- You are more likely to put effort into and achieve goals that are exciting, inspiring and aligned to your values.
- We tend to pay more attention to, and achieve, more demanding goals.
- When we are committed to goals, this increases our ability to attain them.
- It is helpful to break complex goals down into smaller chunks.
- You can boost your self-confidence and sense of wellbeing by embracing microactions.
- Intrinsic goals are linked to higher levels of wellbeing, more autonomy and improved performance.
- Having an internal locus of control can have a positive impact on how you set and pursue your goals.
- If you haven't managed to do something, add the word 'yet' to remind you of the benefits of having a growth mindset.

Putting knowledge into action

Now that you know more about the theories and research around goal setting, how can you apply that knowledge in your life?

Creating a vision

As research shows, having a vision is motivational and helps us decide the steps we need to take to progress towards that vision. Some people like creating a vision board, which visually represents the things they wish for themselves. You can do that on paper or cardboard, using pictures, collage, paint or words. You can also create a vision board using online tools. Make sure it is appealing and exciting to you. Put a picture or a drawing of yourself in the middle of the board and consider all the aspects of your life, such as career, family, friends, relation-ships, finances, health, personal development, or anything else that is significant to you. It is your life, so you get to choose! Then reflect on what you would like to achieve in these areas to create your vision board.

Make sure to include:

- big dreams – those that make your heart sing
- small things, such as exercising daily or walking the dog – think of the things that bring you joy every day.

The vision board is both about 'the trivial pursuits' as well as 'the magnificent obsessions of a lifetime', to use Little's words (1989).

Making space and time for your goals

Once you have a vision, consider your long-term goals (more than 12 months away) and your short- to medium-term goals (between now and 12 months from now). If you don't know what they are yet, that's OK. Write down what brings you joy, or what you want more of in your life.

Then write down your answers to the following questions:

- What are your compelling reasons for wanting to achieve these goals?
- What do you need to accomplish them?
- Do they need to be broken down into smaller chunks?
- What steps can you take right now that will get you closer to achieving these goals?

When you plan your time and your priorities, make sure you give sufficient space for activities that will support you in achieving your goals. If you prefer a more structured way to move towards your goals, you can set up weekly and daily goals and actions. Make sure to include plenty of fun activities to keep you inspired and motivated (see Chapter 10).

SMARTing up your goals

No chapter on goals would be complete without a few lines on SMART. You may have come across the SMART acronym: Specific; Measurable; Achievable; Relevant, and Time-bound. SMART goals help us achieve clarity, enabling us to work out the precise steps we need to take. Despite being a well-known goal-setting technique which has been part of management jargon for decades, not everyone benefits from this approach. Some people prefer a broader and more abstract approach (see Emmons, 1992), while others like to focus on the steps rather than the goal itself. There are no right or wrong ways of setting goals or thinking about the things you want in life. Choose what works for you.

What matters to you?

Setting goals aligned to your values will increase your sense of wellbeing and increase your motivation. Your values are likely to change throughout your life, and according to life events, such as getting married, having children, getting older, and so on. Values are things like health, achievement, success, status, kindness, honesty, love, friendship and family.

One simple exercise to explore your values is to ask yourself the following three questions:

- What are the most important things in my life?
- On a cold, dark morning, what would I get up for?
- What do I live for?

Take your time and list as many things as possible. Then cluster them in similar buckets – for example, success, accomplishment and achievement could go together; kindness, nurturing and caring could go in another one; and so on. Once you have done that, try to pick your top five. The reason for narrowing them down is to help you pin down what truly matters to you. Be aware of those values that are there because you think they are important, and those imposed by family, friends and society. Your values can, of course, be influenced by the environment in which you grew up and live, but it is important to be able to differentiate between the values you truly hold and those which perhaps are 'held on your behalf'. For example, if you study in a competitive environment, 'being first' or 'winning' may be common values adopted by other people; you can then consider whether these are values that truly resonate with you, or not.

Your values act as a compass and when you set goals aligned to your values, you put a virtuous chain in motion which goes like this: you feel good about your goals; because you feel good about them, you put more effort into achieving them; as result, you are more likely to achieve them; you achieve them and feel good about yourself. The result is an increased sense of wellbeing, confidence, self-efficacy and the motivation to create new goals!

Dealing with conflicting goals

Values are also useful when you have conflicting goals – those which cannot be achieved simultaneously or which contradict each other. One example of this is wanting to save money for a holiday versus spending all disposable income on fashion or gadgets. If you split the resource, in this case money, it will take you longer to achieve both goals or it may feel that one or both are somewhat 'compromised'. Choosing how, where and when you spend your time and energy will colour how you experience life. If you find yourself wanting things that are difficult to reconcile, you can always use your values to guide you, and then choose your goals accordingly.

Keeping things in perspective

Goals are designed to serve you, not the other way around. Life happens, things change and so do your goals. Being too focused on achieving goals can lead to tunnel vision, where you lose your sense of perspective. Achieving at all costs can be counter-productive and it can be detrimental to your physical and mental health. Kayes (2006) talks about goalodicy, where our self-image becomes so conjoined with our goals that we find it difficult to backtrack or reroute. As an example, he explains how climbers attempting to summit Mount Everest become so obsessed that they take fatal risks and ignore all the signs that they should not continue their quest.

Final thoughts

Enjoy the journey, but stop now and then to take stock and review your goals in life. Hold on to your dreams, choose well and make sure to find many moments of joy in your daily life to inspire and motivate you.

Six

Look after yourself

Peggy Kern

Introduction

Louisa rubbed her tired eyes. Glancing at the clock, it was 2am. She had to be at work at 8am, but still had another 1,000 words to write. And then there was the upcoming biology exam. Maybe it would be a slow morning at the office so that she could squeeze in a bit more studying. She should have come right back to her flat after class, but Shannon was upset and had needed the support of a friend. 'At least my friends can always count on me', Louisa thought. Still, her studies loomed over her – she couldn't allow herself to get behind. Fighting a rising sense of panic, she pressed on, trying to construct a coherent argument despite the exhaustion she felt.

University life can bring numerous challenges – adjustments to being away from home; trying to make and keep new friends; dating or exploring your sexual identity; essays to write and exams to study for; perhaps working full or part time on the side. How well do you look after yourself in the process? Unfortunately, many of us are not very good at looking after ourselves. Like Louisa, you may be better at taking care of others than you are at taking care of yourself. Maybe it does not seem important. Perhaps it seems selfish to focus on yourself. Or maybe you just don't have the time. Or maybe you're not sure how to. And yet, if we want to not only survive but truly thrive at university and beyond, looking after ourselves is critical.

This chapter explores self-care – what it is, why it matters and how you can integrate it into your life. The good news is that looking after yourself requires relatively little time and effort – simple actions can have big payoffs. By the end of this chapter, you will be able to:

- recognise the toll that ongoing stress can take on your physical and mental health
- define self-care and understand why it matters
- discover simple activities that can be incorporated into everyday life to help you feel and function well
- develop a weekly plan that places your key priorities first, helping you to feel and function well despite any challenges that you might face.

Considering the research

Thriving involves feeling good and functioning well across various areas of life (Huppert & So, 2013; McQuaid & Kern, 2017). Thriving does not mean that challenges and struggle are absent. In fact, many people report having a sense of thriving, despite experiencing numerous struggles (Wellbeing Lab, 2020). This is important, because looking after ourselves can be experienced differently depending on the amount of struggle that we are facing. When life is going well and we face few problems, looking after ourselves involves proactively developing positive habits that support wellbeing. During challenging times, looking after ourselves involves drawing on a variety of coping strategies to effectively navigate the difficulties.

Stress and coping

Regardless of our background and choices, life will be challenging at times. We regularly encounter various stressors – an upcoming exam, sitting in traffic, changing weather, and so on. Sometimes those stressors are particularly intense, such as a major illness or an injury, the death of a loved one, going through a separation or divorce, getting married, starting a job, transitioning to adulthood, or a global pandemic. Large stressors can have a major impact on our health and wellbeing. Still, it is often the accumulation of small stressors that overwhelms us.

Numerous models of stress exist. The classical model suggests that the *experience* of stress occurs when the stressors that we encounter exceed our ability to cope with those stressors (Lazarus & Folkman, 1984). That is, it is not the stressor itself that matters, but our *appraisal* or *perception of the stressor* that results in a physiological and emotional experience of stress. Using an economic metaphor, Hobfoll (1989, 1998) suggested that people have resources that they value (e.g. a house or car, a good job, certain personal qualities, money, power) which they try to conserve and hold on to. People experience stress when those resources are lost or threatened. Carver and Connor-Smith (2010) suggested that stress occurs when we anticipate or experience difficulties in achieving our goals.

Across these views, it becomes apparent that stress arises if we feel *threatened* (we expect there to be bad consequences), perceive *harm* (we believe bad outcomes have already occurred) or feel a sense of *loss* (something that we desire seems like it was taken away) (Carver & Connor-Smith, 2010). For instance, an upcoming exam might be threatening, as your sense of competence is at risk. A past exam might be harmful, as you ruminate on the consequences of failing the exam. You may feel the absence of family as you live away from home. All of these can cause feelings of stress.

Coping refers to the diverse ways in which we respond to threat, harm and loss (Carver & Connor-Smith, 2010). The concept of coping is broad in nature, encompassing a rich history and many views on definitions, categories and approaches (Compas et al., 2001; Folkman & Moskowitz, 2004). For instance, Lazarus and Folkman (1984) distinguished between problem- and emotion-focused behaviours. *Problem-focused coping* directs energy towards the stressor, identifying ways to remove it, avoid it or diminish its impact. *Emotion-focused coping* focuses on the distress caused by the stressor, including behaviours such as relaxing, seeking emotional support from others, crying, screaming, denying the problem and avoiding the emotions. Others point to engaging versus disengaging behaviours (e.g. Moos & Schaefer, 1993; Roth & Cohen, 1986; Skinner et al., 2003). *Engagement coping* involves dealing directly with the stressor itself or the emotions associated with the stressor, whereas *disengagement coping* involves escaping from the stressor or the related distressing emotions (Carver & Connor-Smith, 2010). For instance, mindfulness, seeking support from others, and reconsidering how you think about the event reflect engagement approaches, whereas escaping through substance abuse, self-harm, fantasy and other forms of denial reflect disengagement approaches. Engagement approaches tend to be more useful and productive. While disengagement approaches can reduce the emotions caused by a stressor, they tend to be a short-term solution. They provide temporary relief but are ineffective and often harmful in the longer term.

Coping is often seen as reactive in nature, responding to existing stressors. But coping can also aim to prevent threatening and harmful things from occurring in the first place (Aspinwall & Taylor, 1997). *Proactive coping* tends to be problem focused, identifying potential challenges and actively developing strategies to mitigate or reduce the impact of those stressors. For instance, as you begin the term or semester, you might recognise that you will have a particularly challenging seventh week with several exams and assignments due. You develop a plan to complete the assignments before that week, so that during the seventh week you can focus your attention on studying for and performing well on the exams.

These different forms of coping come together into a distinctive *coping style* – the unique ways that a person copes with different types of stressors (Carver & Connor-Smith, 2010). Coping styles develop from an early age and continue to change and develop across the life span. Just as the internal and external stressors that we encounter in everyday life are varied and diverse, there is not a single right way to cope with challenges – it depends on the situation and the person (Frydenberg, 2017). However, some approaches are healthier, more productive and more adaptive than others. For instance, occasionally playing an online game can provide a useful break from cognitively challenging tasks, but, at other times, the game represents unhelpful procrastination, resulting in short-term pleasure with longer-term negative consequences.

Self-care

Self-care refers to activities that a person purposefully does to care for their physical, mental and social health and wellbeing. These are things such as regularly engaging in health-promoting behaviours, taking time to reflect and rest, and doing activities that make you feel good. It is a *proactive* coping approach, which generally focuses on building positive mental and physical health, rather than treating symptoms of dysfunction. Care is actively undertaken by the self, with the focus on the self (Bressi & Vaden, 2017).

Numerous studies have focused specifically on the intersection of self-care and stress. Within our bodies, the autonomic nervous system (ANS) acts as a control system, functioning largely unconsciously to regulate many of our bodily functions, including our heart rate, digestion and breathing. The ANS has two major divisions: the sympathetic and parasympathetic systems. Stress triggers the sympathetic system, releasing cortisol, priming various bodily functions and preparing us to fight or flee (Cannon, 1932). This is an adaptive response well suited to short-term stressors, such as avoiding an oncoming vehicle or running away from an angry crocodile. The body also wisely self-corrects. As the stressor passes, the parasympathetic system kicks in, dampening the activated response and restoring a normal level of functioning. The body naturally tries to maintain *allostasis* – through which it tries to balance the barrage of internal and external stressors with processes to help us restore stability as we experience change (McEwen, 1993; Sterling & Eyer, 1988). Our bodies are incredibly resilient, with reserves of energy for times of additional stress. However, if stress continues for too long, allostasis becomes harder to maintain; energy reserves are depleted and exhaustion follows. With chronic stress, the sympathetic system is triggered – and remains triggered. Resting heart rate increases, placing pressure on other physiological systems. The body and the mind become increasingly susceptible to breakdown, chronic illness and even risk of early mortality (Friedman & Kern, 2012; Graham et al., 2006; Kemeny, 2007; Segerstrom & Miller, 2004). When chronic stress goes on for too long, it can lead to burnout. Burnout is a form of breakdown, characterised by an overwhelming sense of exhaustion, cynicism and growing detachment from one's work, and increased feelings of ineffective performance and lack of accomplishment (Maslach et al., 2001).

Importantly, numerous studies emphasise the role that self-care plays in preventing and recovering from burnout. Self-care activities trigger the parasympathetic system, calming and restoring us so we are ready for the next stressor. Regularly engaging in simple self-care activities becomes a circuit breaker to the many stressors we encounter. Think about your computer. When you are running many programs at once, it becomes slower and slower until it freezes. How do you fix it? You restart, which clears out the memory and allows it to reset. Computers work more effectively when they are regularly restarted. Likewise, our bodies need to reset, and things like good sleep, moving regularly, engaging in meditative practice, eating well, and so on, help us reset and continue to function well.

Admittedly, self-care is easier when we are feeling and functioning well than in times of difficulty. Think about times when you feel stressed by exams and essays. What happens to your sleep, exercise and diet? For many people, good habits are placed on hold. But these nutrients are vital for restoration and performance. Importantly, we can learn effective coping strategies and establish regular self-care habits that will help us proactively build our wellbeing, as well as successfully navigate the stresses and strains that we encounter.

Summary

Bringing the research together, we know several things that can help us look after ourselves:

- The experience of stress occurs when we perceive threat, harm or loss. Stressors do not necessarily result in the experience of stress; we experience distress when we perceive that stressors exceed our ability and capacity to deal with those stressors.
- Coping refers to diverse strategies that we use to respond to stress. We covered five different types of coping:
  - Problem-focused coping aims to find ways to remove, avoid or diminish the impact of stressors.
  - Emotion-focused coping addresses the emotions that we experience as a result of the stressor.
  - Engagement coping deals directly with the stressors and the emotions that arise.
  - Disengagement coping tries to escape the stressor and its related emotions.
  - Proactive coping focuses on preventing the harm from happening, mitigating or reducing the impact of potential stressors.

- There is no single right way to cope with challenges, as it depends on the person and the situation, but some approaches are better for us than others. Importantly, we can learn effective coping strategies and develop a healthy coping style that will help us navigate stress and challenge well.
- Self-care refers to the activities that we do to look after our health and wellbeing. It is proactive in nature, helps to restore our physiological and mental processes, and reduces the risk of exhaustion and burnout.
- Self-care is often sacrificed in times of stress, and yet it is probably even more important at those times. Self-care is not selfish; rather, it is a way to help us keep functioning at our best.

Putting it into action through I-CARE

How can you make looking after yourself a priority and incorporate it into your busy university life? Using the I-CARE framework can help:

I: We are **Intelligent agents** of our wellbeing through self-care practices.

C: We show **Compassion** for self and others.

A: We are **Authentic** in how we choose to put self-care into action.

R: We are motivated and supported by **Relationships** with other people.

E: We make it **Easy** by using simple strategies that we can incorporate into our busy lives.

Below, we will unpack these elements, providing some simple things you can do to look after yourself effectively.

Importantly, I-CARE requires *caring about yourself*. For some, that will be easy; you believe you have a sense of value and worth, and you want to do what you can to support yourself. However, for others, you may struggle to accept yourself, have low self-esteem and question your worth. If you are struggling, reach out for additional support – trusted friends or relatives, counselling services, your doctor, or others – people who can deeply listen to your story, help you make sense of any difficult experiences you have had, and help you along on your journey. You have much to offer this world, and that begins with recognising your own value.

Intelligent agents

I-CARE begins with us being *intelligent agents* of our own wellbeing. Looking after ourselves is not about blindly following whatever self-help advice we might come across. Rather, it means critically engaging with the research to identify evidence-based approaches that work *for you*. This book provides numerous tools and resources. As you start to practise evidence-based approaches, you'll find what works for you and what does not – empowering you to be an intelligent, active steward of your own wellbeing (McQuaid & Kern, 2017).

Self-care needs to be a priority. We often feel like there is just not enough time in the day for things. But, as intelligent agents of wellbeing, we need to schedule self-care into our everyday life – and this means making it a priority. A simple activity can help us think about our priorities. You can do this as a thought experiment by imagining it in your mind; but it is even better if you can find the materials and try it out for yourself.

ACTIVITY

Learning about goals with rocks

Materials needed: a large jar, some large rocks, pebbles and sand.

Fill the jar part way with sand. The sand represents all the little things that take our attention – time suckers that are not particularly meaningful. Then add the pebbles – these are more important things, but still not what matters most to us. Then add the largest rocks – these represent what we really value and care about. What happens? Often, there's not enough room for all the large rocks. Now get or imagine another jar. This time, place the large rocks in first. With nothing else inside the jar, they fit easily. Then add the pebbles, which fall around the rocks. Then add the sand, which fills in the empty space between the pebbles and the rocks.

Take a few minutes and write down your big rocks. These are the things that are really important to you. You probably will not have many 'big rocks' (perhaps 2–5) and one of them needs to be self-care. Next, think about your pebbles. These are the things that are a priority, but not as important as your big rocks. Now, finally, identify your sand. This is the day-to-day tasks of life that need to get done and the things that take time without delivering much benefit.

Each week, take a few minutes to map out your time. Start with the big rocks (include self-care activities) and then schedule in other things – your pebbles and sand – around those rocks. Then, at the end of the week, review your week. Did you keep your big rocks, or did you allow the sand and pebbles to take over? How can you prioritise your big rocks next week? Over time, by prioritising your big rocks, you'll find that you accomplish more and have more time than you thought possible.

Compassion

Compassion for ourselves and others means that we are aware of the pain of others, feel their suffering, and desire to alleviate the suffering (Wispe, 1991).

We refrain from judgement, simply seeing people as fallible human beings (Neff, 2003). While compassion is often thought of as being focused on others, it can also be directed towards the self. Self-compassion involves being open to our own suffering, desiring to alleviate our own pain, and accepting ourselves as human, despite our failures and inadequacies (Neff, 2003). Importantly, through self-compassion, we are better able to be compassionate towards others.

ACTIVITY

Gaining permission to be human

Have you ever mucked things up? Despite our best efforts, things do not always work out. We live in a society that is averse to failure. We are encouraged to put our best face forward and to hide our inadequacies. Yet we wonder, 'am I the only one who messes up? Why does everyone else seem to have it all together?' Despite all of the images that we can create, we are imperfect and fallible. Self-compassion involves seeing our failings as part of the larger human experience (Neff, 2003).

Think about a situation that went wrong. Take out a piece of paper and answer the following questions, simply free writing:

1   What happened? Describe the details of the situation.
2   What did you do? What were your actions? Do not judge; simply write down your actions.
3   What were the outcomes of your actions? Simply reflect on what resulted from your actions.
4   What did you learn from the situation, and what would you do differently in the future? There are always things that we can learn, insights that are apparent in hindsight. Take a moment to reflect on the lessons that are apparent in your experience, and what you can learn from the experience.
5   How does this reflect your humanity? Consider similar reactions that you have seen in others, recognising that you are human, just like everyone else.

Authenticity

Authenticity is about being true to ourselves. It begins with awareness – knowing who we are (our character, values, strengths and weaknesses, not simply the superficial image that we may portray), what we are feeling and thinking, and how we are behaving. Then, authenticity involves living and acting in ways that honour who we are – not creating an image of what others expect us to be or being the person that others assume us to be, but aligning ourselves to our values and embracing both our flaws and our strengths.

ACTIVITY

Identifying and embracing strengths

We are often better at identifying everything wrong with us, rather than all that we have to offer the world. We all have strengths – some of which are visible and easily accessible, while others are waiting to be discovered. By recognising and drawing on our strengths, our daily activities can become engaging, meaningful and nourishing, rather than boring, meaningless and depleting. Numerous tools are available that can help you start to tune into your strengths. For instance, the Values in Action (VIA) Character Institute offers a free survey, which can help you to explore your strengths and to use your strengths in everyday life (see Chapter 3). Once have identified your top strengths, start drawing on these each day to bring out the best in you and others.

Relating

Humans have a deep need to connect with, relate to and feel a sense of belonging to others (Allen et al., 2018; Baumeister & Leary, 1995; Ryan & Deci, 2000). We are also interconnected with others – our actions impact others, and others impact us (Kern et al., 2020). People in our life provide a reason to look after ourselves, and only by being well ourselves can we help others to be well. Our relationships also provide support. While looking after ourselves is self-initiated, that does not mean that we do everything on our own. Looking after ourselves well means knowing when to reach out for help when we need it.

ACTIVITY

Making use of a helping hand

How good are you at asking for help? Top performers and successful people do not reach success on their own – they have numerous people around them who gave encouragement and support, provided advice or filled instrumental needs at the times that they stumbled, doubted themselves and wanted to quit – and yet we often try to do things on our own.

Take a sheet of paper and trace your hand in the middle of the page. On each finger, write the name of a person that you can seek help from when needed. Outside of the hand, note what each person can help with (e.g. listening to you, cheering you up, providing transportation, sharing information) and why that person is helpful. Then, turn the page over and trace your hand again. This time, list five people or organisations beyond those above that you can go to for help. On the outside of the hand, again note

(Continued)

what sort of help they can provide and why they might be helpful. Hang the hand on your wall, and when you find yourself struggling, consider reaching out to the helping hands around you – and provide a hand to others as they need it.

Ease

There is good evidence to suggest that for change to start and stick, it needs to be made *easy* through simple actions that can easily be incorporated into everyday life. Let's face it: life nowadays is busy. There are many demands on your time and energy. It is easy for self-care to be placed on the back burner, despite good intentions. Indeed, each new year, people make numerous resolutions – how many of them last beyond the first few days or weeks? We rely on motivation and willpower, which quickly fade. Instead, we need simple ways to embed I-CARE into everyday life, such that it becomes automatic and effortless.

──── ACTIVITY ────

Building tiny habits

Consider tiny habits – small actions that seem insignificant, but can easily be done and build a sense of confidence and motivation over time (Fogg, 2020). Tiny habits can be done quickly – even in less than 30 seconds. The action is paired with another behaviour, which becomes a cue to engage in the tiny habit, followed immediately by a reward, which pairs positive emotions with the behaviour. For instance, imagine that you want to start practising meditation. Rather than trying to do a 30-minute meditation, begin with a few deep breaths, tied to starting class. Arrive to a class a few minutes early. Sit down, close your eyes and take a few deep breaths. Then congratulate yourself for completing your tiny habit – use positive self-talk or do a little victory dance. Over time, expand the time or practise in different places. Be flexible and experiment, exploring what works for you, what activities the tiny habit should be tied to, and ways to celebrate.

Final thoughts

Looking after ourselves does not need to be complex, difficult or time consuming, and yet it has big payoffs. Importantly, university is a great time to create regular habits that will support you while studying for your degree and beyond. As stress increases, self-care becomes even more important, for yourself and others.

This chapter has identified why looking after ourselves is important, offering I-CARE as a simple approach to put self-care into action. Thriving does not happen overnight; rather, it is the little things that we do that bring out the best in ourselves and others, despite the stresses and strains that we might encounter along the way. I wish you the very best with your journey.

Seven

Live in the moment

Rona Hart

Introduction

Alice is a very busy first-year student. Having started just a few months ago, she is excited to discover her independence, relishing her first time living away from home. She is meeting new people, making new friends, acquainting herself with the university campus and with the many written and unwritten rules of student life, creating new schedules and routines, and getting to grips with her demanding programme.

Alice is throwing herself into student life with excitement. She studies hard, parties hard and even holds down a part-time job. Time passes quickly because she is busy, and Alice finds that she barely has time to reflect on her new experiences and learning. At times, she is so exhausted that she falls asleep at her desk or finds it impossible to concentrate in lectures. Sometimes, she finds herself not really engaging with her friends or work colleagues as she is worried about the next exam or paper that is due.

At times, she has a sense of being on a rollercoaster ride, not really in control of what is happening to her. She worries that spreading herself too thinly may undermine her learning and achievements. She wishes that she could disembark from this fast ride, just to take stock and evaluate everything that is happening. She would prefer to enjoy what she is doing rather than worrying about the next task.

Her university offers a mindfulness course for students and a friend invites Alice to participate. Alice is reluctant to take on yet another obligation, especially one that requires daily practice. She has little idea what mindfulness is and would like answers to her questions: What is mindfulness? What does it take to practise it? How would it benefit her?

These are the questions that this chapter will address.

Mindfulness

Mindfulness seems to be everywhere today – in schools, universities, hospitals, workplaces and even government institutions. For some, it is considered therapy; for others, technology. Many people see it as a lifestyle choice. Mindfulness is practised by millions of people in the West, and by even more people in Eastern cultures. In public discussions, it is sometimes presented as a mystical panacea – a cure for all the ills of modern societies. Regrettably, with its growing popularity, many myths and misconceptions have emerged.

In what follows I aim to offer an overview of mindfulness: what it is, how to practise it, what it is useful for, and its potential benefits based on research evidence. Along the way, I shall de-mystify some common myths and misconceptions.

After engaging with this chapter and its activities, you will have:

- an overview of mindfulness: what it is and what it means to be mindful or mindless
- an awareness of the common myths and misconceptions of mindfulness
- an understanding of how to practise mindfulness: What is formal and informal practice? What is meditation and how is it practised? What constitutes the optimal practice of mindfulness?
- a glimpse into the vast research into mindfulness and an understanding of its therapeutic power: When is mindfulness the right solution? What are its potential benefits? What are the challenges of mindfulness?
- some exercises that you can easily apply to gain its benefits.

The Eastern approach to mindfulness

The mindfulness approach discussed here was developed by Jon Kabat-Zinn and his associates in the 1970s. It draws on Buddhist meditative practices and is therefore considered an Eastern approach to mindfulness. Within Buddhism, the practice of mindfulness signifies a higher level of conscious awareness. As it was adopted in advanced, industrialised nations, the practice became 'Westernised', downplaying its religious and spiritual content, thereby creating a non-religious therapeutic-contemplative practice. This is how mindfulness is practised and offered to this day. It is considered therapeutic in its orientation since it is used to alleviate a range of physical and psychological conditions.

Exploring mindfulness

Drawing on Buddhist philosophy, Kabat-Zinn defines mindfulness as 'paying attention in a particular way: on purpose, in the present moment, and non-judgmentally' (1994, p. 8). Mindfulness entails observing *external* events as well as *internal* experiences as they occur (Baer, 2003). When we pay attention to internal events, we may observe our thoughts, our emotions or body sensations as they occur. Focusing our attention on external events means attending to anything that is going on around us that is captured by our senses: any sights, noises and events.

Kabat-Zinn's definition suggests that mindfulness entails:

* self-regulation of attention
* directing our attention to internal or external experiences
* metacognitive consciousness
* adopting an accepting, non-judgemental attitude.

One of the biggest misconceptions around mindfulness is that it is a state that occurs when meditating. Mindfulness is in fact a state that we employ many times in our everyday lives. Every time we pay attention to something, it can be said that we are being mindful. So, you already know how to be mindful! Kabat-Zinn (2003) clarifies that mindfulness meditation is a training method that aims to enable people to extend periods of mindfulness into their everyday lives.

Mindfulness and 'mindlessness'

Mindfulness is often contrasted with 'mindlessness'. Mindlessness can be described as a state of superficial awareness, where we rely on automatic thoughts, habits or behaviours to perform tasks. In short: it is when we are on autopilot. Mindless repetition can be used to develop expertise and peak performance.

ACTIVITY

Exploring the differences

Do you have a driving license? If you have, can you recall how you felt when you drove for the first time after passing your test? Were you vigilant, stressed, cautious, excited?

Now try recalling how you felt a few months later. Maybe relaxed, enjoying the drive, able to eat, speak, or make a to-do list in your mind while driving?

In our first week of driving once we have passed our test, it is likely that we will be in a mindful state. Every bit of our attention would be focused on our driving techniques

(Continued)

and skills. Compare that with a few months later. Through practice, our driving skills have become habituated and automated. We can therefore drive 'mindlessly'. It is like we are on autopilot, and we are able to multi-task because driving no longer requires all of our attention. This is what we refer to as a mindless mode. It occurs when we reach a fairly high level of competence. This shift between mindfulness and mindlessness occurs every time we learn a new skill.

The difference between the mindful and mindless mode of attention is linked to another misconception around mindfulness. There is no expectation that we should be mindful all the time. This is neither possible nor desirable. Both mindful and mindless modes are required in life. We constantly shift between them. Indeed, being on autopilot from time to time is important for conserving energy and when doing something that requires expertise. However, research suggests that many of us spend *most* of our time in autopilot mode (Kabat-Zinn, 1994). This very high level of mindlessness is harmful to our wellbeing because we tend to make more errors and have more clashes and accidents when we are in autopilot. Kabat-Zinn (1994) argued that the result of this habitual state of shallow attention is an undisciplined mind that becomes an unreliable instrument for examining internal or external processes.

The key message of mindfulness research and practice is that we need *more balance* between the two modes to maintain optimal wellbeing in our lives. For most of us, this would mean being more mindful and spending less time in autopilot mode.

The goal of mindfulness practice, therefore, is to develop a disciplined mind (Kabat-Zinn, 2005), through increased capacity to self-regulate our thinking. In a sense, mindfulness offers us a tool to control our minds. This is gained through a variety of mindfulness practices, including meditation, which are explored below.

The qualities of mindfulness

Mindfulness practice entails three essential qualities (Shapiro et al., 2006):

- practitioners' *intention* in mindfulness practice
- directing *attention* to internal or external experiences as they transpire
- the *attitudes* that meditators bring to mindfulness practice.

The *intention* in mindfulness practice addresses the questions 'why do we practise?' and 'what are we aiming to achieve through practising mindfulness?' Research suggests that the intentions of practitioners tend to vary across several categories (Shapiro et al., 2006):

- relaxation or self-soothing of the mind or body
- self-regulation – control over the self

- self-exploration – knowledge of the self
- self-liberation – transcendence of the self: being able to connect to higher goals, to reach enlightenment or to become more spiritual.

Many people start their mindfulness practice with an intention to relax and reduce stress. For some, this may move on to different intentions. Interestingly, research outcomes correlate with these intentions.

There are six elements that make up *attention* (Brown et al., 2007):

- being present-focused
- having clarity as to what one observes
- being non-discriminatory
- having flexibility of awareness and attention
- taking a value-free stance towards our experience
- gaining stability of attention.

Research suggests that practitioners gradually develop these qualities through practising mindfulness.

The *attitude* feature may contain some or all of the following qualities (Shapiro et al., 2005):

- not judging: neutrally observing the present moment
- acceptance: recognising and embracing things as they are
- letting go of thoughts, feelings or experiences
- patience: letting things progress in their own time and at their own pace
- gentleness: having a soft, considerate and tender outlook
- being open-minded: considering things anew or creating new possibilities
- empathy: understanding another person's state of mind
- not striving: not forcing things and not aiming to achieve an end
- trust: having confidence in oneself and in the processes unfolding in life
- generosity: giving without expecting anything in return
- gratitude: being thankful
- loving kindness: caring for others, forgiving and loving unconditionally.

These attitudes are very powerful and are at the heart of mindfulness practice. Mindfulness training is designed to help people bring these attitudes into their mindfulness practice and into their everyday lives.

Mindfulness interventions

In 1979, Kabat-Zinn and his colleagues developed and launched the Mindfulness-Based Stress Reduction (MBSR) programme at the University of Massachusetts

Medical School. MBSR is a group-based intervention that trains participants to practise mindfulness regularly so that they can become more mindful in everyday life. Many of the programmes offered today in healthcare, education and workplaces are based on the original MBSR structure, contents and principles.

MBSR includes:

- 8–10 weekly group meetings, in which participants are offered mindfulness instruction and practice, yoga exercises, group discussions and individual support
- participants being expected to practise mindfulness at home (40–60 minutes per day) – this daily practice is crucial for attaining the benefits of this training; about 40 minutes per day is considered optimal practice time, though recent studies have found that just 10–15 minutes practised consistently can deliver significant benefits (Creswell, 2017)
- often, an intensive silent mindfulness meditation retreat (for a day or two) (Didonna, 2009).

MBSR is widely available today. It is usually offered in group settings facilitated by a trained mindfulness instructor, either face to face or online through video-conferencing technology. It is also offered in a self-help (non-facilitated) mode through books, video or audio programmes or through mobile phone apps. The facilitated face-to-face and live video-conferencing delivery is showing much better results than video or audio lectures, books or apps, mainly because dropout rates from the non-facilitated programmes are substantial (Gál et al., 2021).

MBSR was initially developed as an add-on treatment for patients experiencing chronic pain (Kabat-Zinn, 1982). Over the years, MBSR has been successfully tested on many other physical and mental conditions (Ivtzan & Hart, 2015). Today it is offered by several national health services (e.g. the National Health Service (NHS) of the UK) to patients diagnosed with cancer, heart disease, and varied chronic illnesses (such as fibromyalgia, high blood pressure, asthma or skin disorders). It is also offered to patients experiencing a variety of psychological symptoms, such as stress, depression, anxiety, panic, post-traumatic stress disorder (PTSD), sleep disturbance or fatigue. The goal of MBSR is to reduce physical and psychological ailments through the enhancement of patients' self-regulatory capacities, which are developed through the daily practice of mindfulness exercises (Kabat-Zinn, 2003).

——————— POINTS FOR REFLECTION ———————

Minding pain

MBSR was inspired by Buddhist meditation retreats, which often require meditators to practise for hours while sitting motionless. Although practitioners naturally adopt a comfortable position, the prolonged stillness often results in pain in muscles and joints.

Meditators are encouraged not to change position to ease the pain, but instead to consciously focus on and attend to the ache sensations, and the thoughts, emotions or urges that arise, while adopting a non-judgemental attitude towards them. The ability to observe painful sensations with acceptance is believed to ease the distress provoked by it since it promotes the awareness that pain and the feelings that accompany it are 'just thoughts' and are not reflections of truth or reality, and thus do not necessitate escaping or avoiding them (Baer, 2003). Kabat-Zinn (1982) claimed that the prolonged exposure to pain, without catastrophising it, can lead to a reduction in the emotional reactivity triggered by the pain, thus leading to desensitisation, which in turn eases the pain.

Kabat-Zinn et al. (1992) described a similar mechanism for relieving psychological disorders, such as anxiety and depression. They claim that repeated attentiveness with an accepting attitude to troubling thoughts or emotions, without escaping them, can reduce the emotional reactivity, and thereby relieve symptoms. The assertion of MBSR is therefore that, with repeated practice, practitioners can become skilled at being less reactive towards their symptoms, whether the symptoms are physical or psychological, and thereby better able to restrain adverse patterns of thinking and behaviour (Shapiro et al., 2006).

MBSR includes two types of mindfulness practice:

- *formal practice*: different types and lengths of meditation practice
- *informal practice*: everyday mindfulness; this is when we bring mindful attention to an everyday event – mindful walking, mindful eating, mindful cooking, etc.

It is important to practise both regularly to get the desired results. Therefore, the 40-minute daily programme mentioned earlier is made up of both formal and informal practice.

ACTIVITY

Trying a breathing meditation

Sit comfortably in your chair with your back supported well by the chair. Try to sit up, but only to the point that it is still comfortable and not an effort. Place your feet on the floor and your hands on your legs. When you are comfortable, close your eyes.

Listen to the following recording: https://youtu.be/_m-KfN6k4Kw

'As you are sitting comfortably and closing your eyes, I'd like to invite you to become aware of your breathing. Simply focus on your breathing and become aware of it. Breathing in ... Breathing out ... Breathing in ... Breathing out ... Take note of the pace and depth of your breathing. Take note of the air as it flows in and out, through

(Continued)

your nose to your lungs, and note your belly expanding and contracting ... Simply be with your breathing ... Not trying to change anything, not trying to control your breath ... just let it be, as it is. Breathing in ... Breathing out ... Breathing in ... Breathing out ... Breathing in ... Breathing out ...

If your mind wanders, and your attention goes away from the breath, when you notice it, gently go back to focus your attention on your breath. Do this gently, kindly and non-judgementally ... Accept with grace and compassion that your mind has wandered and escort it back to the breath when you notice. Breathing in ... Breathing out ... Breathing in ... Breathing out ...

When ready, slowly come back to the here and now.'

Mindful movement

This is when we bring mindful awareness to any activity that we do in everyday life. Therefore, when cooking, washing dishes or taking a shower, instead of having a vivid conversation with our boss, friend or mother-in-law in our head while doing the activity, the invitation is to pay attention to the activity itself and fully be with that experience.

ACTIVITY

Developing mindful attention

In the mindful movement practice (adapted from Stahl & Goldstein, 2019), you are invited to bring your full attention to the movement of the body. Stand up and follow the instructions as best you can. If you have a physical difficulty, consult your physician or physiotherapist before embarking on this exercise. Go to the following link to start the practice: https://youtu.be/gZbwHPjMBCA

'Stand in bare feet or socks, with your feet a bit apart and more or less parallel to each other. The back is straight, but not stiff, shoulders relaxed, and hands are down by your sides.

It is important to be gentle with yourself as you do these stretches, applying self-care during the movement. Let the wisdom of your body decide how far to go with any stretch and how far to hold it. You are invited to see this practice as a chance to cultivate awareness of the body as you carry out these gentle movements.

As you are standing here, notice the contact points between your feet and the floor. Try to distribute your weight evenly between both feet, unlocking the knees so that the legs can bend slightly. See how this feels. Breathe naturally. Then on an in-breath, slowly and mindfully raise both your arms to the sides, so they come to be parallel to the floor. And just breathing here for a moment ... And then inhale and continue to raise your arms slowly and mindfully until your hands are raised above your head, with the palms facing each other, stretching upwards.

Ground yourself on the floor, as you breathe in, and stretch up like this for a few breaths …

And then when you are ready, slowly, on the exhale, begin the journey back. Allow the arms to come down, breath by breath … Tune into the changing sensation as the arms move … Until the arms come back to rest.

And now, breathing naturally, stretch your right arm up over your head, as if you are picking a fruit from a tree. Bring your attention to the sensations that are felt through the body, and be aware of what the breath does as you stretch.

And now, allow the left heel to come off the floor as you stretch, keeping the toes on the ground. Feel the stretch right through your body. Breathe naturally … And now, allow the heel to come back to the floor. Begin to lower your hand, following the fingers with your eyes if you choose. Notice what colours and shapes your eyes capture as they follow your hand. And now when you face the centre, tune into the after-effects of this stretch, along with the sensations of the breath …

Now, breathing naturally, stretch up to pick fruit with your left hand … Then, allow the right heel to come off the floor to help the stretch. Once again, notice what parts of the body are involved in this stretch. Just become aware and let go of even the smallest tendency to push beyond your limits … And now slowly and gently, allow the heel to come back to the floor … The arm returns slowly to your side, following it with your eyes all the way if you choose. Let the arms come back to rest. Allow the face to come back to the centre, and tune into the after-effects of this stretch, along with the sensations of the breath …

Now place your hands on your hips and very slowly and mindfully on an out-breath, allow your head and shoulder to bend over to the left, with the hips moving a little to the right, so the body forms a curve that extends from the feet to the hips and torso, bending sideways.

Breathe in … It's not important how much you bend, it is the quality of attention that you bring to the movement that matters. And on the in-breath come back to stand straight and remain here for a moment.

And then repeat the same movement to the right side. On the out-breath, put your hands on your hips and gently and mindfully allow your head and shoulder to bend over to the right. And breathe in with this … And now, on the in-breath come back to standing straight, and remaining here for a moment, breathing in.

And finally do some shoulder rolls. First, raise your shoulders towards the ears, then move the shoulders backwards, and then let the shoulders drop down, squeezing the shoulders together in front of the body. And then put these movements together in a smooth, rolling motion – up, back, down and forward. Let your breathing pace determine the speed of the rotations so that you are breathing in for half a movement and breathing out for the other half.

And now change it, so that the shoulders move in the other direction.

And now coming to stillness, standing here, aware of sensations in the body, the after-effects of doing these stretches, and the sensations of the breath moving in and out of the body.

As we come to the end of this practice, congratulate yourself for taking the time to be present.'

Meditation

Meditation is one of the key training practices included in MBSR. But what is meditation and how does it help us become more mindful in everyday life, and develop a disciplined mind?

Meditation is defined as 'a family of techniques which have in common a conscious attempt to focus attention in a non-analytical way' (Shapiro, 1980, p. 14). The goal of meditation practice is 'the development of deep insight into the nature of mental processes, consciousness, identity, and reality, and the development of optimal states of psychological well-being and consciousness' (Walsh, 1983, p. 19). The aim of meditation is to alleviate suffering by developing metacognitive awareness and self-regulation of attention and thought (Wallace, 2005). The deeper level of perception that is exercised during meditation is a mode of being that meditators aim to bring into their daily lives (Olendzki, 2009).

The common meditative techniques can be divided into three main types (Shapiro et al., 2005):

- *Concentrative meditations*: in concentrative practices, practitioners attempt to control their attention by focusing on a single object or idea, while ignoring other internal or external stimuli. Awareness is thus focused on the object of meditation – which could be one's breathing, a mantra, a word, a phrase or a sound. Mantra meditation, loving-kindness meditation and transcendental meditation (TM) are considered concentrative techniques (Siegel et al., 2009).
- *Mindfulness meditations* are considered mental practices for opening up attention. The objective is not to select a particular object to focus on, but to notice the shifting experiences (Siegel et al., 2009). In mindfulness practice, practitioners attempt to notice whatever predominates their awareness in the moment – internally or externally. They are taught to bring an attitude of openness, acceptance and kindness to observed experiences, and to avoid evaluating, criticising, altering or attempting to stop these experiences, even when they are taxing (Baer, 2003). Zen meditation is an example of a mindfulness practice.
- *Contemplative meditations*: these types of meditations involve appealing to a larger spirit (a higher power, such as a deity) while accepting a state of not knowing. From this position, practitioners may ask questions and bring up unresolved issues. Contemplation is more commonly practised as a spiritual practice than in a therapeutic context.

It is worth noting that within MBSR and similar training programmes, the meditation practices include a combination of mindfulness and concentrative techniques.

For example, the breathing meditation offered earlier is concentrative because it entails concentrating on our breath. More advanced meditation practices included in MBSR often start with a concentrative technique (such as focusing on the breath) and then move on to mindfulness techniques where meditators are asked to observe whatever is happening in the moment (e.g. bodily sensations, thoughts or emotions). This is because researchers have found that concentrative techniques can facilitate mindfulness practice (Shapiro et al., 2003).

How does meditation lead to the development of a disciplined mind?

Most meditations involve a dynamic process of monitoring our awareness and regulating our attention. When we engage our minds with meditation, it is common for us to find our mind wandering. There is only one instruction in meditation: when your mind wanders, bring it back. Therefore, when noticing your mind wandering, gently come off your new train of thought and bring your attention back to your meditation with acceptance and tolerance. It is important not to scold ourselves or think that we are doing it wrong. That is what minds do – they wander. This cycle of mind-wandering and bringing back the attention to the instructions of the meditative practice repeats itself numerous times in the space of one practice (Olendzki, 2009). Thus, the essence of the process is not the contents of consciousness, but the process of managing it (Didonna, 2009). According to research, this process is one of the key mechanisms of mindfulness, as it provides a powerful exercise for the brain. By doing this repeatedly, we learn to control our attention. Research suggests that our ability to control our attention promotes and develops our capacity to self-regulate our thoughts, emotions, behaviours and even bodily sensations (Didonna, 2009).

An additional key mechanism that makes mindfulness effective in reducing physical and psychological disorders is that it changes our relationship with our thoughts, emotions and bodily sensations (Shapiro et al., 2006). This mechanism involves a paradox: on the one hand, it entails becoming aware that we are continuously flooded by a river of thoughts. By practising mindfulness, we develop a very close relationship with ourselves, gaining a better understanding of our thoughts. Similar awareness is developed around our emotions and bodily sensations. On the other hand, we learn not to get caught up in these thoughts, emotions or sensations. This is known as *dis-identification* – being able to disidentify from your own thoughts, emotions or sensations as if you are a person watching from the outside looking in (Shapiro et al., 2006).

—————————————— ACTIVITY ——————————————

Learning to STOP

There are several meditations as well as informal practices that enable us to develop the capacity to disidentify from our own thoughts, emotions or sensations. The following brief informal practice invites us to bring our awareness to internal events such as thoughts, emotions or bodily sensations, allowing us to re-balance our mind and body after a challenging or stressful event.

The following practice is called STOP (adapted from Stahl & Goldstein, 2019). It consists of four steps:

- S = Stop
- T = Take a breath
- O = Observe
- P = Proceed.

There may be times during our busy day when we are unaware of what is happening inside us. By taking just a brief moment to stop, take a breath and discern what is happening, including our own thoughts, emotions and sensations, we can reconnect with our experiences, balance our emotional state, and then proceed and respond more effectively. This practice can be very illuminating. You may discover that you are experiencing a pain in your shoulder, that your jaw is clenched, or that you are sitting uncomfortably. You may also notice that you are hungry, tired, stressed, frustrated or anxious. You can practise this STOP activity any time you feel stressed or upset. Once you notice where you are, you can acknowledge, accept, release tension and rebalance. You might choose to do this practice before or after certain activities, or you may even schedule in various times during the day to STOP and check in with yourself. With this activity, you can become an active participant in the management of your own psychological wellbeing and develop the capacity to experience the present moment, no matter how difficult or intense, with more balance and peace.

Research on mindfulness interventions

In the past 50 years, extensive research has been conducted to examine the psychological and physiological effects of mindfulness training and therapies. The research suggests that mindfulness programmes can improve a variety of physical and psychological conditions. Many of these studies focused on MBSR. Several interventions combine mindfulness with cognitive behavioural therapy (CBT). A leading example is mindfulness-based cognitive therapy (MBCT) (Segal et al., 2002). This was originally designed to prevent relapse in patients with a history of depression, but has also been trialled successfully with other disorders such as anxiety (Chiesa & Serretti, 2011).

There is a substantial body of research on mindfulness programmes amounting to thousands of papers. The summary below offers a glimpse into this vast literature. Several studies found that the electrical activity of the brain is responsive to mindfulness training, prompting a rise in beta activity (associated with wakefulness) alongside increased alpha and theta waves (both of which are generated in a state of relaxation) (Chiesa & Serretti, 2010). A number of studies found that after a few weeks (4–8) of mindfulness training, certain areas in the brain are not only activated more often but also show changes in the constitution and performance of the brain. The areas shown to be affected are associated with pain, emotion, consciousness, attention, cognition, self-awareness, introspection, memory, sensory and visual processing, and the regulation of emotional or behavioural responses (Chiesa & Serretti, 2010; Marchand, 2012). Further research has shown that mindfulness training induces a state of physical rest, as measured by respiratory and metabolic performance, blood pressure and cortisol secretion (Marchand, 2012). Mindfulness training offered to participants with cancer found that it strengthened their immune function (Witek-Janusek et al., 2008). Several studies examined the effects of mindfulness when delivered in educational settings (mainly schools and universities). These studies revealed that mindfulness training can improve learning skills: short- and long-term memory functions, attentiveness, perception, curiosity, concentration, metacognitive awareness, cognitive flexibility, imagination, creativity and inventiveness (Marchand, 2012). Several clinical trials have demonstrated a significant decline in subjective pain experience following mindfulness training (Chiesa & Serretti, 2010; Grossman et al., 2004; Kabat-Zinn et al., 1992). MBSR was also shown to improve skin condition in patients with psoriasis (Kabat-Zinn et al., 1998); and resulted in improved sleep and reduced fatigue in cancer patients (Shapiro et al., 2003).

In psychology, mindfulness training can significantly lower symptoms of psychological distress, including anxiety, panic, worry, stress, depression, suicidal ideation, self-harm behaviours, rumination, neuroticism, anger, cognitive disorganisation, thought suppression, post-traumatic stress disorder and substance abuse (Keng et al., 2011). Mindfulness training has shown to be effective in reducing symptoms of bipolar disorder, social phobia, psychosis, dissociation, borderline personality disorder and eating disorders (Chadwick, 2014; Kristeller & Wolever, 2010; Williams et al., 2008; Zerubavel & Messman-Moore, 2013).

Improvements in wellbeing following mindfulness training include: increases in happiness, life-satisfaction, psychological wellbeing, quality of life, positive emotions, hope, sense of coherence, sense of control, autonomy and independence, coping skills, resilience, moral maturity, spirituality, self-actualisation, self-compassion, stress-hardiness, emotional regulation, self-esteem, self-acceptance, benevolence, trust, empathy, forgiveness, the ability to express emotions, improved social relationships and social adjustment, and even a better sense of humour (Friese et al., 2012; Keng et al., 2011; Robins et al., 2012). As can be seen from this brief overview of the research, mindfulness practice is showing impressive outcomes and I therefore encourage you to try to engage with these exercises daily.

─────────────── ACTIVITY ───────────────

Practising a loving-kindness meditation 1

To end this chapter, I invite you to try out this loving-kindness meditation (adapted from Stahl & Goldstein, 2019). You can follow the recording provided here: https://youtu.be/1bFOMice-yc

'Begin your practice by congratulating yourself that you're dedicating some precious time to meditation. As you begin to become present, become aware of the body and mind and whatever is carried within you. Simply allow and acknowledge whatever is within you and let it be ... without evaluation or judgement. Gradually, shift your awareness to the breath, breathing normally and naturally. Breathing in, breathing out ... Just being aware of your breathing ... Just living life, one inhalation and one exhalation at a time. Breathing in, breathing out, watching each breath appear and disappear. Just breathing.

Now gently bring awareness to your beating heart, feeling any sensations within and reflecting on how fragile and precious life is. The heart is the gateway into deeper compassion and love for yourself, and for all beings. Now feel into your own precious life with compassion, mercy and love. Feel into the powerful qualities of loving kindness itself, a boundless, altruistic love that can be compared to the sun, the moon or the stars, shining on all living beings without distinction, separation or prejudice. Bring this love into your own heart, skin, flesh, organs, bones, cells and being. May you open to deep kindness and compassion for yourself, recognising and accepting the imperfectly perfect being that you are. It may be a struggle to feel love towards yourself. Work with this by acknowledging your challenges, and then continue to open to discover what it feels like to have an experience of loving kindness towards yourself. Take a moment to be open to each of the following phrases for a few minutes, letting them sink into your being:

- May I be safe
- May I be healthy
- May I have ease of being
- May I be at peace.

Now expand the field of loving kindness to one or many benefactors, teachers, mentors and others who have inspired you, repeating the same phrases:

- May they be safe
- May they be healthy

- May they have ease of being
- May they be at peace.

Now gradually expand the field of loving kindness to one or many near and dear ones among your family, friends and community:

- May they be safe
- May they be healthy
- May they have ease of being
- May they be at peace.

Now further extend the field of loving kindness to one or many neutral people, acquaintances and strangers:

- May they be safe
- May they be healthy
- May they have ease of being
- May they be at peace.

Now consider extending loving kindness even to one or many of those difficult people in your life. It may seem challenging or even impossible to send loving kindness to this group. With the understanding that resentments have a toxic effect on your own health and wellbeing, begin to neutralise them by sending loving kindness and compassion to yourself. Then reflect on forgiveness and realise that conflict and unkindness often have their roots in fear and lack of awareness. Open your heart and extend loving kindness to your rivals, and then further extend the wish that they will find the gateway into their own hearts, gaining greater awareness and transforming their fear into love. Gently and slowly send loving kindness to these enemies or difficult people in your life:

- May they be safe
- May they be healthy
- May they have ease of being
- May they be at peace.

Now take some time to remember those less fortunate, bringing into your heart anyone you know who is experiencing physical or emotional pain. Picture these people who face difficulty or challenges experiencing more healing and peace. Further expand this circle of healing to all beings. May all living beings experiencing sickness in the body or anguish in the mind be at peace. Now send loving kindness to all who are victims of natural disasters or war, and to those who are hungry or without a home. May they too be at peace. Extend loving kindness to anyone who is feeling anxiety, stress, isolation, alienation or hopelessness, and to those who are addicted or lost or who have given up. May they too be at peace. Letting none be forsaken, may those who are suffering in any way be at peace. Build this loving-kindness energy to become as boundless as the

(Continued)

sky and begin to radiate it to all human beings and all living beings. Send loving kind-ness to all living beings, omitting none, whether great or small, weak or strong, seen or unseen, near or far. Send this vast love to all beings of the earth, the water and the air, spreading loving kindness in all directions:

- May all beings be safe
- May all beings be healthy
- May all beings have ease of being
- May all beings be at peace.

As you begin to withdraw from the loving-kindness meditation, come back to the breath, and sensing and feeling into the whole body as you breathe in and out. Feel the entire body rising upward on an inhalation and falling downward on an exhalation. As you come to the end of this meditation, may you share any merits you've gained with all beings. May all beings be at peace.'

Final thoughts

Mindfulness is:

- an opportunity to turn off our autopilot system, connect with our lives and be more present
- a mode of attention and awareness that we already have
- a way to develop self-awareness, acceptance and self-compassion – it can help us become more aware of our own thoughts, emotions and bodily sensations, learn to accept them as they are, and respond non-judgementally and compassionately
- a method that enables us to alleviate a variety of mental and physical health disorders, including stress, anxiety, depression and pain
- a way to develop resilience and avoid creating additional distress for ourselves during difficult times
- a means to develop the capacity to self-regulate our thoughts, emotions and behaviours, and to learn to relate to events in our lives with less reactivity and a gentler and more non-judgemental attitude
- a way of being with yourself and others that conveys loving kindness, and is empathetic, altruistic, trusting and caring
- a way of being that can bring increased wellbeing and wisdom
- evidence based: there is significant research around its benefits.

Mindfulness is *not*:

- a quick fix that can take away all your troubles or stressors; mindfulness requires consistent practice and effort to see its benefits
- a practice that requires you to empty your mind, or be mindful all the time, and does not occur only when meditating
- a one-size-fits-all approach: people tend to develop their own unique way of practising mindfulness; also, it does not suit everyone, and it does not work for all. It should therefore not be forced on others
- a panacea: although mindfulness can alleviate mental and physical disorders, it should not be used as a substitute for medical treatment or psychological therapy – oftentimes, it may be used by medical and psychological professionals as an add-on to treatments
- an all-or-nothing type of experience – you can indeed join a training programme, try it out and engage with it as little or as much as you wish, and slowly build up a habit of practising
- a practice that distances you from life, helping you to escape from difficult experiences, or from your memories or emotions – in effect, it allows you to engage with your experiences more intensely, and work through them with acceptance and self-compassion.

Ultimately, you are the only person who can decide if mindfulness is suitable for you, how it fits into your life, or whether it is helpful. If you have an opportunity to try it out, I'd recommend taking it. My hope is that you will find enough in this chapter to intrigue you and encourage you to have a go and try it out. The practice of mindfulness offers a path of discovery that can help us create new ways of being, doing and interacting with others. We may discover new possibilities, as well as befriend ourselves in the process.

Eight

Invest in relationships

Aneta Tunariu

Introduction

Relating to other people, whether on a temporary basis to serve a distinct goal (e.g. collaborating with classmates to secure a comfortable seat for the duration of a lecture), or longer term (e.g. making friends), is a large part of our everyday lives. In fact, a considerable proportion of our emotions and moods involves other people. Relationships are part of our everyday ups and downs. They aptly demarcate life's natural milestones as well as its planned and unplanned opportunities for remarkable personal development. The capacity to form and sustain positive relationships is pivotal to both vibrant social organisations and the thriving inner world of the social actors that inhabit these – you! It is widely understood that university life offers a particularly unique, exciting and rewarding social canvas for connecting with like-minded people – sharing learning, co-creating memories and establishing lifelong friendships.

This chapter will examine relationships, consider why they matter and discuss ways to cultivate and practise *positive relating*. We will explore how positive relationships are good for your wellbeing and vitality, for your personal growth, and for building valuable social capital for the future. In alignment with the ethos of the book, the intention is to raise your aspirations for personal fulfilment and enrich your natural capacity to relate to self and others out of fullness and through graceful giving.

Meaningful relationships

The study of close relationships and interactions with significant others has long been a preoccupation of philosophers, social and developmental psychologists, psychologists studying personality, and health practitioners interested in the therapeutic aspects of positive relationships. Close relationships tend to involve regular exposure through consecutive interactions between individuals with shared goals and connected frames of reference. Characterised by transactional sharing, disclosure and meaningful connections, close relationships play a significant role in our lives as they afford experiences known to shape our personal journey in some way – during our formative years as well as in adulthood. For instance, research shows that our sense of closeness and belonging, relational satisfaction, emotional dispositions, ability not to respond defensively to failure, and overall personal wellbeing are enhanced when we experience people in our relationships as responsive. This positive impact of 'partner responsiveness' relates to the extent to which we feel they understand us, are attentive in ways that validate our experience and care for us (for a review, see Selcuk et al., 2019).

At times, in everyday conversation we find ourselves speaking of relationships as if they were 'a thing' – a 'bubble' that envelops two or more people. Notwithstanding the acknowledgement of a shared contour, this terminology can be misleading as it suggests that relationships are something that 'happen to people' or that once they happen, they just are – static and self-perpetuating. However, if we take the time to think about it, we see that from the beginning and throughout, relationships are punctuated by a lively process of information exchange and multi-modal feedback filtered through the lenses of personal beliefs, needs, expectations, real-time emotional states and situational motives (see e.g. Reis & Rusbult, 2004). Rather than being something separate and static, this *process* of relating takes place between actively participating individuals, each with their own *subjective* views and style of 'giving' and 'accepting'. In other words, a relationship unfolds through and because of the dynamic *intersubjective* space created by what individual participants consciously and unconsciously contribute (add in) and receive (take out). Hence the common expression: what we (can) 'take out' from a relationship is greatly shaped by what we (choose to) 'put in' to it. Acknowledging our active role in determining and co-creating both the quality and experience of a relationship is an important and empowering orientation towards mature relating and self-mastery (see e.g. Becker, 1992; Feeney, 2007).

Meaningful relationships are those that have an impact on us. They may be *close relationships*, such as those with our parents or siblings, other caregivers or family members, friends or romantic partners. Likewise, they may include *time-bound professional alliances* involving people, who, for instance, we relate to in a mentoring way (e.g. a facilitator at the student support services).

These relationships differ based on the nature of activities involved, the degree of mutual disclosure, and so on, but share a key characteristic: namely, the possibility of encountering affirmation, joy and contentment alongside frustration, disappointment, rupture or hurt. This is an important tension and dichotomy to recognise. At the heart of whether a close or meaningful relationship is 'good' is its ability to allow and hold the space for discomforting events and experiences to unfold, long enough to acknowledge and address them constructively and equitably. The degree to which this is possible is indicative of whether a relationship is limiting and holding back positive living; or enabling, acting as a catalyst for positive living. Before we go deeper and learn about some of the habits of thought and action that help promote positive relationships, let's examine some of the key theories about relationships and their place in the human condition.

Why do we have a need to be in relationships?

Research suggests that relationships are critical to help us develop, adapt and thrive. At the core of the human fabric, it matters to us that we are socially accepted; we seek this recognition and respond positively to its presence. This is one of several core social motives that have evolved to help us survive as social beings living in organised communities. Social psychologist Susan Fiske (2018) synthesised over 60 years of psychological research on relationships and found five overarching interconnected social motives that are responsible for energising and directing our focus and investment to form and maintain meaningful relationships. A mixture of cognitive and affective motivations, the five core social motives are: belonging, understanding, controlling, enhancing self and trusting others. They can be remembered as BUCET if we pronounce it as 'bucket'.

Belonging

We have a fundamental need for belonging in relationships and groups as it ensures physical and psychological survival through the safety, comfort and lowered anxiety provided in strong and stable relationships. Visible and invisible culture rules curate 'belonging' and set guidelines for the actions we might take to feel or prove that we belong. Experiencing meaningful, deep connections or light, joyful encounters with people that we choose to be with goes a long way to addressing and satisfying this motive as we replenish our knowing that *there is a place for us, just as we are*; a recognition that helps to strengthen our sense of self.

Understanding

This is a fundamental need to understand other people and be understood by others. In understanding others with ease, we become able to relate to their goals and wishes, and to predict their intentions. It enables collective frames of reference to emerge and sets foundations for collaboration and co-existence, both of which are important for surviving and thriving.

Feeling understood extends the need for shared meaning and shared reality and is a complex and deep-seated motive. It encompasses being seen by another person in such a way that we feel recognised, known and accepted. In being seen in this way, our individuality is honoured and our uniqueness accepted. This recognition helps strengthen our sense of being 'special' and deserving. It is not surprising, therefore, that we tend to connect with and enjoy the company of people who 'get us' and whom we 'get'. The way to open ourselves up to this is a simple act of looking at and seeing another from a place of respectful curiosity and openness.

Controlling

This is a fundamental need to feel competent and effective at managing our social environments, our boundaries and ourselves. We are motivated to manifest and come to see our actions as having an impact. In other words, we like to think that we can make a difference and accomplish our intended outcomes. When we do, this lowers our anxiety and inspires confidence that continuity and order, not chaos, will characterise the future. When we don't, we become more sensitive to social cues and preoccupied with information gathering as a way of seeking to (re)establish control. As Fiske (2018) puts it, the belief in the value of control 'describes how people make sense of each other, how certain attitudes are retained, how people feel initially attracted [to each other, or not], and how relationships can cause emotions' (p. vi).

It can be easy to think of the term 'control' with negative connotations and so dismiss it. Consider, however, how the application of skills for effectively conveying our needs, asking for a certain kind of help or pitching a proposal in a persuasive way are forms of social control that can and do help guide positive and rewarding relationships. In other words, when others come to assist us to realise our goals, we feel effective and get a sense of being in control. In turn, they would have grasped our intentions and chosen their response. In this way, their own social motives of understanding, contributing and controlling are met.

There is, of course, the question of dependency. Autonomy shines an important light on the idea of control as a social motive for investing in positive relationships. Both dependency and autonomy are in themselves necessary and unavoidable. Tension and discomfort arise when one is either in overdrive or under-compensated. Yet, new possibilities and insights tend to show up in this type of 'it's outside my comfort zone' scenario. When we step back and take perspective, we note the seemingly paradoxical status of these two contrasting positions (see also Feeney, 2007) and realise that, in accepting their interdependence, we can then experience *the rhythm underpinning positive relating*. Perhaps Arthur Schopenhauer's (1850s) 'porcupine parable' made prominent by Sigmund Freud in the 1920s, helps capture the natural enabling rhythm at the heart of human relating: namely, we seek to achieve a balance between 'closeness' and 'autonomy' that best promotes flow and movement and prevents stagnation and disconnection (cf. Luepnitz, 2002). In the porcupine parable, a group of porcupines are grouped together on a cold winter's day. To keep warm, they try to share body heat by moving closer together. However, as you can imagine, when they move closer together to huddle for warmth, they start to poke each other with their quills. In turn, in order to stop the pain from each other's spikes, they then move away again and spread out, thus losing the warming advantage of being close and so begin to shiver. This brings them back to the beginning and they start to get closer again, the cycle repeating as they try to find the best distance to achieve warmth without pain.

Enhancing self

This core social motive refers to a fundamental need to expand – that is, to come to know ourselves and to actualise our potential. The self-expansion model of motivation (Aron et al., 2013) helps explain some aspects of our dominant constructions of and attitudes towards social success and personal fulfilment, values and goals, and the aesthetics of friendship and of romantic intimacy. According to this model, and the large body of research that supports it, close relationships naturally fulfil the human need and disposition to expand, through assimilating our partner's beliefs, perspectives, knowledge (including their insights about ourselves) as well as aspects of their social identity, and other social capital and resources. All being equal, this process is paralleled by an ongoing reciprocal process of 'including the other in the self', focused on motivating and replenishing the other partner in the dyad. Choosing what relationships to invest in, and *knowing why this matters for both participants*, are important topics for our inner dialogue on living a fulfilling and purposeful life.

Validation from other people boosts our own internal self-validation repertoire of resources and reliably scaffolds self-esteem, self-care and self-belief (see also Mashek & Aron, 2004). The reverse is also possible – negativity or scarcity of validating actions from certain people in our lives can deplete our internal resources and cultivate self-doubt. In those cases, we may find ourselves being troubled by negative thoughts: Do I belong? Am I deserving? Am I capable? While we like and care for people who make us feel good, we are not always necessarily deliberate about letting this guide who we spend time with or expend emotional energy over. Relationships with individuals that leave us with the pleasant and energising sense of 'they bring out the best in me' are the ones we ought to invest in.

Trusting others

This is a powerful need that connects across all core social motives. Trusting others is the foundational pre-requisite for self-disclosure, interdependence, commitment and attachment. Propelled forward by a leap of faith, we assume a position of openness and act with confidence that those who we are interacting with are benevolent. The expectation of a fair and compassionate world of people creates an open and curious mindset and, all being equal, inspires the same in return. Disclosure and revealing can feel like a 'risk'; it can provoke us into feeling vulnerable or sensitive to being misunderstood, to rejection or ridicule. Yet, we gain most self-insight when we 'reveal' ourselves to others. An existential perspective can be helpful here – for us to muster the courage to be (to become; to live a full life), *'risk' and a commitment to taking creative positive actions* are required (Tillich, [1959] 2014).

In summary, core social motives 'describe fundamental, underlying psychological processes that propel people's thinking, feeling, and behaving in situations involving other people' (Fiske, 2018, p. 12). They are generated by the interplay between person and situation, human nature interacting with social conditions, rather than being a matter of personality disposition. Each one of us, albeit with various degrees of similarity, experiences the drive of these five core social motives. The more we are aware of their significance, the more we can align our actions to our higher-order values and invest in establishing and nourishing the kind of relationships we would like to have.

Attachment

In addition to the five core social motives proposed above, it is important for us to consider the concept of attachment. Attachment is the strong affectionate bond through which the self seeks to be close and connected to another. It is a key feature of meaningful relationships, entangled in complex ways with trust and trusting. Attachment in adulthood may mirror and repeat the dominant attachment style of our childhood when initial patterns of relating and attachment dynamics began to shape our sense of self (see e.g. Mikulincer & Shaver, 2007). Put simply, the main attachment styles (secured, preoccupied, dismissing, fearful) are based on internalised models of self and of others. *Who am I?*

The response tends to draw on heavily invested narratives about the self as positive or negative, self-reliant or dependent, and so on. *Who are other people?* This response tends to draw on heavily invested narratives about others as positive or negative; trustworthy or untrustworthy; to be avoided or to be encountered. (For more on attachment styles in adult intimate relationships, see Feeney, 2008). Key to note here is that what we (consistently) tell ourselves matters most. For instance, when our answers to the question *Who can I be in the presence of others?* do not get re-examined regularly as we grow in maturity, then we are stuck rehearsing narratives of the past as the reality of the present. This would represent a missed opportunity to become aware of the values and self-beliefs that best capture ourselves today. We are always catching up with ourselves. Examining and, as/where necessary, upgrading the narratives we tell ourselves are fundamental to *successfully managing the self-attunement gap* – the ebb and flow of the extent to which we know and positively lead ourselves.

Positive relating: The self and others

Positive relating can be described as an enabling orientation characterised by openness, fluidity, non-intrusion and honest and thoughtful dialogue. It leads to relationships capable of holding conditions optimal for an individual to 'stand out' (differentiation); optimal for an individual to expand (intentional witnessing); and optimal for both individuals to connect (belonging, trusting). One way to understand how the self and others can relate is through the 'I-It and I-Thou' lens proposed by Martin Buber ([1923] 2004).

I-It or I-Thou

Buber identifies two modes of relational existence: *I-It* or *I-Thou*. A relationship understood as *I* to *It* involves an attitude of objectifying and minimising the value and significance of the other. In this case, the *I* is privileged at the expense of non-relating, not recognising, disaffirming the other as an *it*. The *it* is conceived of and comes to be experienced as an object: predictable, fitting the value and attributes that are projected onto it. On the other hand, a relationship understood as *I* to *Thou* involves an attitude of mutual recognition of agency and significance of the other. Both the *I* and the *Thou* are recognised as subjects, with subjective realities, preferences and needs. Both are entitled to choices and to exercise these in the shared relational space. The *Thou* is conceived of and comes to be experienced as a mindful being, who is whole and affirmed as such. Positive relating encapsulates living meaningfully in *I* to *Thou* relationships.

—————— POINTS FOR REFLECTION ——————

Rules of thumb in positive relating

- What we tell ourselves matters: there is much to gain from monitoring self-talk.
- How we 'love' ourselves matters: it sets the bar and signals our expectations about how we wish to be treated by others.
- Relating involves encountering: choose to cultivate an open, curious and non-judgemental style of meeting yourself and others; in this way, we may learn something valuable every day and are more likely to avoid rehearsing taken-for-granted views and their inherent circularity.
- Relating involves giving: give to others from a place of plenty (rather than from a place of need, e.g. needing to prove a point or expecting a certain outcome); in this way, chances are that there is no room for regret, or feeling our 'giving' was not fully valued.
- Relating involves giving: give to yourself in good faith; when in doubt, trust your intention – What would you like others to see when they encounter you today? How would you like to be treated?

—————————— ACTIVITY ——————————

Considering meaning

What thoughts cross your mind when you read these quotes?

- 'Whenever you're in conflict with someone, there is one factor that can make the difference between damaging your relationship and deepening it. That factor is attitude.' (William James)
- 'Nobody can hurt me without my permission.' (Mahatma Gandhi)

The skill of noticing

- What we tell ourselves matters most: we can monitor self-talk. One way of developing a greater sense of agency and allowing us to achieve greater clarity is to become better at noticing. To put it simply, noticing can help us to 'become conscious of additional information that might be helpful' (van Nieuwerburgh, 2020, p. 65). Noticing with curiosity and without anticipating or judging can be a powerful tool to master.

---------------- **ACTIVITY** ----------------

Thinking of a close friend

As you think of a close friend, respond to the five questions below without too much deliberation. The first thought that comes to mind tends to offer useful insights.

Overall score: the minimum is 5 and the maximum is 25. The ideal score is between 15 and 20.

1 I enjoy the company of this person:
   1 (to a little extent) – 5 (very much so)

2 I can be 'silent' yet not feel alone in their company:
   1 (to a little extent) – 5 (very much so)

3 I feel 'heard' and understood by them:
   1 (to a little extent) – 5 (very much so)

4 I find it easy to listen to and support them every day:
   1 (to a little extent) – 5 (very much so)

5 I know that we will resolve tension or disputes openly and with mutual closure:
   1 (to a little extent) – 5 (very much so)

---------------- **POINTS FOR REFLECTION** ----------------

10 practical strategies for positive relating

1 Be thankful: show and express gratitude to others on a daily basis.
2 Be available: ensure that you carve out time regularly for relationships that matter to you.
3 Be respectful: acknowledge and appreciate differences and respect people's needs.
4 Be affirming: make sure to acknowledge the people in your relationships. Make time to listen to them. Show empathy when they talk about their experiences.
5 Be trusting: assume the best in others. Avoid jumping to conclusions. If there is reason to be doubtful, check with them first.
6 Be curious: notice what is happening in your relationships. Keep an open mind and make sure that you do not take others for granted.
7 Be accountable: remember to treat others the way they would like to be treated. Be clear about how you expect to be treated.

(Continued)

8   Be positive: find opportunities to focus on the strengths of others. Help to counterbalance negative emotions and remind others of their resourcefulness.
9   Be giving: give with grace and do the right thing for the relationship, setting aside any preoccupations with 'being right'.
10   Be forgiving: be prepared to let things go. We all make mistakes.

POINTS FOR REFLECTION

Reparative conversations – Speaking from the heart

Sometimes positive relationships may be damaged for various reasons. In these cases, take steps to repair the relationships as soon as possible. One way of doing this is by 'speaking from the heart'. A process for doing this is presented below:

1   Communicating thoughtfully:
     • speak without offending, listen without defending

2   Acknowledging:
     • speak about the actions (words, behaviour, etc.) that were subjectively experienced as hurtful
     • listen to individual subjective realities without minimising or dismissing these

3   Taking ownership:
     • stay long enough with the moment to gain insight
     • stay long enough with its emotions to take ownership of the contribution one has made to causing the hurt or the unpleasant emotions

4   Moving forward – the possibility of reparation:
     • express remorse and offer sincere apologies
     • contribute to making sense of the past and co-authoring the future while being present in the 'here and now'.

Final thoughts

The aim of this chapter was to offer theoretical and practical scaffolding for the invitation to invest in acquiring the skill of noting and experimenting with positive relating, and to help you appreciate the importance and benefits of investing in meaningful relationships. Two notable drives at the heart of the human condition are having a purpose and making a contribution (see e.g. Boniwell & Tunariu, 2019). Through their ability to enable and validate, positive relationships in our lives are fundamental to both these drives. In meaningful relationships, *purpose* is facilitated through self-expansion, actualisation and other affirming opportunities connected to the five core social motives discussed earlier in this chapter. For instance, feeling 'seen' in the right way honours our individuality and difference and helps strengthen our sense of being 'special' and deserving. This powerful gift of positive relating is highly dependent on the quality of partner responsiveness. In meaningful relationships, *contribution* is facilitated by opportunities for giving to and serving others. It addresses our social motive to belong as well as offering the grounding sense of being needed. Individual moment-by-moment experiences of positive relating have self-affirming and gratifying properties. Cumulatively, these experiences come to form our internal resources for self-validation, self-soothing, grit and resolve to move forward. Getting the art of relating right may not always be uncomplicated but will always be worth it.

Nine

Prepare for adversity

Hanna Kampman

Introduction

I would like to start by inviting you to take *a deep breath in*. This simple action can do wonders to calm our bodies and minds – often needed when facing difficult times. I will additionally write something that perhaps is not the most traditional way of starting a chapter: feel free to skip this chapter. Sometimes, if you are in the middle of dealing with a significant life challenge, just reading about this topic can be distressing. That is understandable. Listen to yourself and how you are feeling. If now is not the right time, come back to this chapter later when it feels right for you.

Dear Nietzsche, could you clarify something?

For most of us, life is a combination of beautiful highs and challenging lows, with some quite comfortable stages in between. Going to university can be exciting, daunting, intellectually and socially demanding, and many more feelings besides. It is likely that during your time at university, you will face various types of hardship as well. 'Prepare for adversity' is a strange title to have for a book chapter because adversity tends to be impossible to prepare for. Often, that is its nature: unexpected and raising questions about the way you view this life. This makes adversity something that we do not wish to prepare for. However, I hope to show you that you can surround yourself with resources to help you when you encounter these troubling life situations. Perhaps, you may even recognise the positive transformation that can potentially ensue from severe adversity.

There are various perspectives you could take on how to *prepare for adversity.* Many of these are addressed elsewhere in this book (e.g. looking after yourself in Chapter 6 and live in the moment in Chapter 7). This chapter will focus on two psychological concepts that lend themselves to this topic area: *psychological resilience* and *post-traumatic growth.*

In this chapter, psychological resilience is defined as a dynamic process *before,* *during* and *after* adversity, leading to a positive adaptation (Chmitorz et al., 2018; IJntema et al., 2019). This means that resilience can be, at times, the ability to stand strong in the face of adversity or the ability to recover relatively quickly with minor impairment, and often in some way strengthened and more resourceful. Most importantly, resilience entails the wisdom to know when to stand strong, and when to accept that we have been hurt and need to recover.

Every so often, reality comes even closer, and we are challenged to contemplate life and the way we view it at a fundamental level. These events, that often 'shatter our assumptions' about ourselves and the world, can be extremely difficult and even traumatising (Janoff-Bulman, 1992). Even these starkly confronting experiences sometimes hold space for transformative growth. This phenomenon, most often referred to as post-traumatic growth (PTG), is seen as both a process and an outcome. PTG is defined as positive transformative changes resulting from a struggle with a highly challenging life circumstance (Tedeschi et al., 2018). In this chapter, these changes are seen as both action-oriented (Hobfoll et al., 2007) and embodied (Hefferon, 2012; Hefferon & Kampman, 2020; Hefferon et al., 2009). This means that the change will show in the way you think, behave and in your relationship with your body.

The concepts mentioned above are regularly present in our everyday language. Many of us have heard Nietzsche's famous words: 'that which does not kill us, makes us stronger'. We might have also heard that 'smooth seas do not make skilful sailors', or well-meaning people suggesting to us that we should have more 'grit'. There are also times in our lives when we may feel that we have reached our maximum levels of strength, and we have no desire to become stronger: 'No more challenges, please – the strength and conditioning have been quite enough at this point, thank you. If the sea requires such a skilled sailor, perhaps it is better to stay on land'! In other words, in times of adversity, some of these popular sayings might be difficult to take on board and may perhaps even be hurtful amidst a traumatic experience. Therefore, I want to emphasise that the chapter you are reading is only an invitation to explore these concepts – it is not meant as a prescription. I want to share these ideas, as many people have found hope and strength from them or even recognised something that they are already experiencing and exhibiting in their lives but never had the words for.

This chapter will:

- define adversity and acknowledge how common it is
- define resilience and post-traumatic growth as well as awaken the wisdom to know when to lean into each one
- help you to recognise and foster resilience and post-traumatic growth in your life by inviting you to undertake several activities.

I come in peace, only armed with research

This chapter particularly addresses the severe challenges of life, times that can even be traumatising. There is no clear consensus among researchers when it comes to defining adversity in relation to psychological resilience. Rather, adversity can entail various things, from small everyday stressors to significant adverse events (Bryan et al., 2017; IJntema et al., 2019). What appears to be more generally agreed on is the notion that our subjective understanding of adversity is an essential element of this definition. In other words, what is highly stressful for one individual might not be as distressing for someone else. Your evaluation of the situation matters: What is happening here? Can I handle this? Do I have the resources to handle this? Our previous experiences also matter: the first time we fail an assignment, our first failed romantic relationship, or our first time being fired from a job can all be devastating because we have not experienced them before. Thus, we might appraise the magnitude of the event strongly, consider our resources to deal with it as lacking and view the implications as being far reaching.

The adversity or trauma in PTG is defined as 'a highly stressful and challenging life-altering event' (Tedeschi et al., 2018, p. 4). These events have 'a seismic impact on individuals' worldview and functioning' (Tedeschi et al., 1998, p. 2). A metaphor of an earthquake is sometimes used to describe how a trauma shakes the foundations of the individual's worldview (Tedeschi et al., 2018). For PTG, adversity entails both objective and subjective aspects. This means that most people would find the situation highly stressful, and your personal reaction entails severe distress and helplessness. I often refer to trauma as a thief – it steals some aspects of your life (e.g. a job, a part of your identity, a sense of security, hobbies, or friends). Even if the traumatic event(s) were similar between two people, what it takes from someone is always personal. We should consciously respect everyone's individual journey and be kind towards ourselves if we appear to be struggling where someone else is not. It is worth mentioning at this point that the potential growth journey following these struggles will be unique as well.

Resilience: To bend or not to bend?

There is a lovely tree metaphor for different ways of defining psychological resilience (Lepore & Revenson, 2006). Some trees bend amidst the storm, recovering quite quickly back to their original position. This type of resilience is often referred to in the literature as *recovery resilience* (Lepore & Revenson, 2006) – the ability to rebound or bounce back. Individuals exhibiting recovery resilience will have minor or short-term disruptions to their wellbeing and will quite swiftly return to their previous level of functioning (Fletcher & Sarkar, 2016). It is important to note that the recovery resilience does not suggest that the individual has not been affected by what has happened (Zautra et al., 2010). You might have had a hard, unpleasant time which you do not wish to experience again where you are not able to do things as before. This is only temporary though and you are feeling yourself quite quickly after the situation has passed.

There are also trees which stand strong in the storm (Lepore & Revenson, 2006). This type is known as *resistance resilience*, or standing strong in the face of adversity. Individuals exhibiting resistance resilience will maintain their previous level of wellbeing and performance despite the hurdles (Fletcher & Sarkar, 2016). Zautra, Hall and Murray (2010) describe this type of resilience as sustainability – the capacity to keep going. You might be exhibiting resistance resilience when facing hardship yet still being able to engage with life, as usual, and enjoy what you are doing. You are attending to the difficulties and perceive that you have the resources and ability to deal with them.

Finally, some trees might bend and accommodate the storm; however, instead of returning to their previous shape, they somehow adjust. *Reconfiguration resilience* can be seen in individuals as an ability to rebound from adversity stronger and more resourceful (Walsh, 1998). When defining resilience this way, it is akin to PTG, enabling 'recovery and positive growth' (Walsh, 2012, p. 399).

Sometimes standing strong is an option and can help you to get through difficult times. However, standing too strong for too long can be exhausting. Often, the smartest thing to do is to admit that we need help. A break, rest and recovery are only possible if we acknowledge that we need them. Resilience is the wisdom to know the difference and act accordingly.

PTG: A ray of hope

The term 'post-traumatic growth' was first used in the mid-1990s by Richard Tedeschi and Lawrence Calhoun (1995). This phenomenon stemmed from clinical practice worldwide, where practitioners witnessed that even after the most harrowing experience, people often expressed benefits that they perceived they had gained from the journey (cf. Joseph, 2012). These positive changes were truly transformative for those individuals who had 'developed beyond their previous level of adaptation, psychological functioning or life awareness', meaning they had grown (Tedeschi et al., 1998, p. 3). Currently, these transformations are seen as positive cognitive, behavioural, emotional and even biological changes that an individual may experience in the aftermath of a traumatic event (Tedeschi et al., 2018). It can be witnessed in how people view themselves, among their relationships and in their philosophy of life. It is essential to understand that it is not the event itself from which the growth stems. Rather, PTG evolves as the individual is working hard to come to terms with the aftermath of their trauma. This can take years as the person purposefully acknowledges and accepts the losses, carving space for new insights. PTG is not about reactive and quick changes immediately following traumatic events. The gradual changes are part of a lengthy and unfolding journey (Tedeschi et al., 2018; Tennen & Affleck, 1998). The process of cultivating growth demands new ways of 'thinking, feeling and behaving' because what has happened does not allow the individual to 'return to baseline functioning' (Tedeschi et al., 2018, p. 5). This means that those individuals reporting PTG surpass the previous levels of functioning in some ways.

People reporting PTG often have common themes in their growth outcomes (cf. Hefferon & Kampman, 2020; Kampman et al., 2015; Tedeschi et al., 2018):

- an appreciation of life
- personal strength
- an ability to relate to others
- new possibilities
- spiritual and existential change
- a new awareness of the body.

Individuals who have gone through significant adversity often say that they *appreciate their life more*. People might talk about enjoying the little things more, which they took for granted before. Because adversity often questions us in ways that we could not imagine, we might even develop a sense of *personal strength*. People often describe this as 'if I can survive this, I can face anything'. Sometimes we start appreciating the people in our lives more and *relate to others* differently. Individuals talk about knowing who their true friends are and who truly matters in their lives, valuing these relationships and putting more effort into maintaining them. *New possibilities* might arise and be recognised after the experience, such as opportunities for a new career (e.g. public speaking) or engaging with new hobbies that are meaningful (e.g. sports) (Kampman & Hefferon, 2020). Going through trauma can often remind us how small we are in this vast world. People reporting growth, on the other hand, talk about being part of something larger than themselves – humanity (Kampman et al., 2015). Therefore, *spiritual and existential change* are common outcomes of dealing with adversity. Finally, a very physical trauma, such as severe illness or injury, might awaken a more embodied experience of PTG that leads to *a new awareness of the body*. Individuals reporting corporeal PTG discuss acknowledging and appreciating their physical being more, and being kind towards their bodies (Hefferon, 2012; Hefferon & Kampman, 2020; Kampman & Hefferon, 2020; Kampman et al., 2015). Several studies have shown clear similarities in individuals' stories (Tedeschi et al., 2018), with growth experiences circling around the themes mentioned above. Still, the growth achieved following adversity is always as unique as you are.

Stephen Joseph (2012) describes growth after trauma with an illuminating vase metaphor. Joseph suggests that there are times in our life where a treasured vase gets knocked down. The vase breaks on impact; however, you can still put it back together as it was. You will probably see the cracks, but it is still the same vase. It might even be stronger than before, depending on how it was attended to. But sometimes in life the impact is so strong that the vase breaks into smithereens. It is no longer possible to rebuild the vase as it was. With time though, you can build something uniquely beautiful from the remnants: a mosaic.

Summary

- Most of us will face adversity during our lifetime, thus it is normal to struggle at times.
- Adversity is always personal. What is highly stressful for one person might not be so for someone else.
- Psychological resilience is a dynamic process involving an interplay between various factors: adversity, context, individuals' reactions, and individual and environmental resources.
- As a dynamic process, psychological resilience can be facilitated through learning and activity.
- PTG is both a process and a potential outcome of the struggle with adversity.
- Individuals might experience growth in one area of life and not in others.
- It is completely normal not to experience PTG.

The following section will offer some ideas on attending to 'our unique vase'. The section is built to offer something to you, whether you are in the process of fixing the vase or piecing together a mosaic. I do want to remind you that each activity is an invitation – you do not need to engage with them if it feels too much for the time being.

Putting this into action

As with any skills training, it is better to practise a skill before you need to master it. Because of this, my first recommendation is to read and engage with the other chapters in this book. Some of the best-known facilitators of psychological resilience and PTG are covered in other chapters of this book. Start by looking after yourself (Chapter 6) and identifying your strengths (Chapter 3) that guide you in this life. Engaging in these activities can increase your resources and help you focus on what brings you vitality, meaning and positive emotion. Being playful (Chapter 10) is a serious matter that can connect you to your meaning. Spending time with your friends, doing something fun, can additionally reduce your levels of stress while you have more positive feelings. In fact, one of the most common resilience and PTG facilitators is meaningful relationships (Long & Bonanno, 2018; Tedeschi et al., 2018) (see Chapter 8). You can, additionally, increase your personal resources by focusing on what is possible (Chapter 5) and learning through doing (Chapter 2), as both perspective-taking and learning from past challenges are at the centre of resilience. Living in the moment (Chapter 7) is an ideal approach for grounding yourself in the present. In the midst of adversity, hope (see Chapter 4) can be an essential forward-moving force (Yıldırım & Arslan, 2020). Finally, those individuals who report PTG often talk about moving from a self-centred perspective to caring about the world (Chapter 13) and the other people in it (Kampman et al., 2015).

Due to this book already being a roadmap to resilience and a potential facilitator of PTG, I will focus on some of my personal favourites in this chapter. We will be spending time in nature and I will also help you to think with kindness. Additionally, we will aim to capture the learning and to recognise growth in your life.

Facilitating resilience

When it comes to psychological resilience, it is essential to know what type of resilience we are facilitating (IJntema et al., 2019). The following suggestions are divided into activities according to the type of psychological resilience. It is also important to consider where you are in your resilience journey: before, during or after (IJntema et al., 2019). The other chapters in this book are fantastic resources to familiarise yourself with, *before* you find yourself in the middle of adversity. The following section will therefore focus on the periods *during* and *after* the adversity. Two interventions are proved to be most effective in facilitating resilience: mindfulness (see Chapter 7) and cognitive-behavioural techniques (Joyce et al., 2018). The following activities will therefore lean on these two concepts.

--- **ACTIVITY** ---

Grounding yourself with the help of nature

One of the key tenets of mindfulness is grounding yourself in the present moment (Hart et al., 2013; Ivtzan & Lomas, 2016; see also Chapter 7 in this text). Two things are likely

(Continued)

to happen when dealing with hardship. Our mind is drawn towards the past, and we tend to become sad because of what has happened. Equally, our mind might drift into the future, and we can become anxious about what might happen because of the situation we are in. Luckily, nature has a wonderful ability to offer 'soft fascination' for us – it can hold our attention without demanding it (Duvall & Sullivan, 2016; Kaplan & Kaplan, 1989). The following exercise can be beneficial for facilitating resilience (as well as for carving out space for PTG) as it helps you ground yourself in the present moment.

This activity is based on a tested positive psychology intervention by Hamann and Ivtzan (2016) and on research around attention restoration theory (ART; Basu et al., 2019; Duvall & Sullivan, 2016; Kaplan & Kaplan, 1989). ART suggests that there are four ways nature can restore our attention (Duvall & Sullivan, 2016, pp. 38-39): by offering a chance for *being away* from mentally tiring activities and environment; surrounding ourselves with something that *fascinates* us without effort; offering a vast space where we will have a feeling of *extent*; and through *compatibility* between the activity and what you are trying to take a break from:

- Spend at least 15 minutes a day in any type of outdoor or natural environment; if interested, try walking, running or cycling to move your body as well.
- Turn off your electronic devices.

When choosing this place, ask yourself the following questions:

Being away: Where can you be away from mentally tiring activities? What could potentially distract you there? Can you leave these items behind?

Fascination with: What for you is effortlessly fascinating? Can you find a place which offers you this soft fascination? What holds your attention but does not demand it?

Extent of: Where might you feel a sense of extent, a feeling of space? Where can your mind freely drift into its surroundings?

Compatibility with: How is your break compatible with what you are trying to have a rest from? How could you make the restorative environment differ significantly from the mentally tiring environment?

If your mind still wanders – which is what minds often do – try the following:

- Focus on one thing that you can see; what are its colours, shape, depth?
- Move on to finding one thing that you can hear; is it soft, sharp, does it have rhythm?
- Finally, focus on your body and notice what you feel in your body; is it tension, softness, cold, warm?

These activities aim to give you a break from rumination and the environment which might be distressing you. These activities can calm your nervous system, allowing you to feel a bit more relaxed and centred, often enabling you to see more clearly and discover new perspectives and resources.

Cognitive-behavioural therapy (CBT)

CBT was pioneered by Aaron Beck in the 1960s and is centred around the idea that our thinking, feeling and behaving all impact each other. More specifically, how we think about a situation influences how we feel about it, which has implications for the actions we choose to take. As you may remember, cognitive, emotional and behavioural aspects are at the centre of the dynamic process of resilience, making CBT techniques an ideal tool to increase our potential for adapting to challenge in resilient ways.

———— ACTIVITY ————

Engaging with your thinking patterns

The following exercise aims to engage with your thinking patterns to see if you might be engaging in some unhelpful ways of thinking. Most of us have some thinking errors which we are not aware of. When our reflection is not accurate, it can lead to inaccurate feelings about the situation, leading us to act accordingly. In Table 9.1, I have listed some commonly recognised thinking errors. See if some of them resonate with you. If so, acknowledge that they are thinking errors. Also, consider other interpretations. I have set aside space for you to write on the pages of this book.

Table 9.1 Thinking errors and how to correct them

Thinking errors	What is happening?	How does this thinking error show?	Can you think of a different, more adaptive interpretation?
Catastrophising	We think that one thing leads to another, with a worst possible outcome which we are not going to be able to cope with	This one mistake will mean that *I will get fired*	Everyone makes mistakes. I have many qualities that make me good at my job; I just need to practise this one aspect more
Write down your personal example and adaptive interpretation of Catastrophising			

(Continued)

Table 9.1   (Continued)

Thinking errors	What is happening?	How does this thinking error show?	Can you think of a different, more adaptive interpretation?
All-or-nothing thinking	'Either/or thinking' involves exaggeration of outcomes: fail or succeed, good or bad	I failed this assignment so *I will not graduate*	I have passed all other assignments so the likelihood is that I will graduate; perhaps I did not work hard enough *this time*, so next time I will start earlier
Write down your personal example and adaptive interpretation of All-or-nothing thinking			
Fortune telling	Thinking that we know the future and outcome of the event(s)	*I know I will fail* this exam	I do not *know* that I am going to fail; what *I do know* is that I can take the test and find out
Write down your personal example and adaptive interpretation of Fortune telling			
Mindreading	Believing that we know what others are thinking and assuming the worst	Everyone *will think* that I am not very smart because of this presentation	I cannot possibly *know* what people think; they could just as well think the opposite – I could request feedback on this presentation
Write down your personal example and adaptive interpretation of Mindreading			
Overgeneralisation	Using words such as everyone, everything, always, never – suggesting that the context of the situation does not matter	Bad things *always* happen to me	A lot has happened lately, and it makes me *feel* that only bad things happen; if I take a bigger perspective to things, a lot of good has happened too
Write down your personal example and adaptive interpretation of Overgeneralisation			

Thinking errors	What is happening?	How does this thinking error show?	Can you think of a different, more adaptive interpretation?
Labelling	Giving yourself negative labels, talking to yourself negatively	I failed my essay, so *I am* a failure	This time I did not succeed in my goals
Write down your personal example and adaptive interpretation of Labelling			
Demands	Expecting how you should always feel and behave, causing anxiety and disappointment	*I should* already feel better, *I should* not make mistakes, *I must* control my feelings	I am a human being. I can be sad or tired sometimes, people who do not make mistakes probably do not do anything at all
Write down your personal example and adaptive interpretation of Demands			
Tunnel vision	Focusing on one aspect and ignoring all the other information	This *one* person in the audience appears really bored of my presentation, so *I must be doing a bad job here*	Perhaps this one person is tired or has something else on their mind, as the rest of my classmates appear to be enjoying this
Write down your personal example and adaptive interpretation of Tunnel vision			
Minimising versus maximising	Includes minimising the positive significant events (e.g. achievements) and/or maximising the significance of negative events (e.g. a failed essay)	I am on *my third year of university* which is not anything special – I failed one course, on my third year, which defines my whole degree	I should celebrate my achievement so far! Let me consider all the assignments I have completed so that I can appreciate how far I have travelled
Write down your personal example and adaptive interpretation of Minimising versus maximising			

(Continued)

Table 9.1   (Continued)

Thinking errors	What is happening?	How does this thinking error show?	Can you think of a different, more adaptive interpretation?
Personalising	Thinking that you are the sole reason behind negative events, you might feel guilt and shame	*It is my fault* that nobody is having fun at this party	Maybe not the best jamming session but there are 20 other humans here equally responsible for the atmosphere
Write down your personal example and adaptive interpretation of Personalising			
Externalisation	When you are not taking responsibility for your role in your situation, it can cause inaction (helplessness) and feeling that you are not in control	*The university is causing* me to fail my assignments	Maybe I could reach out more to understand the assignments: Have I used all the resources given to me? Have I allocated enough time to work on my essays?
Write down your personal example and adaptive interpretation of Externalisation			

It is powerful to recognise your erroneous thinking patterns so that you can start questioning them. What is the worst thing that can happen due to the situation you are in? If you look back on this, will it matter in five years' time? Particularly take notice if you are using superlatives such as 'always' or 'never', and consider whether they represent reality.

I recommend listening to this song: 'What a Difference a Day Makes', performed by Dinah Washington and written by Maria Grever and Stanley Adams:

'What a difference a day made

Twenty-four little hours

Brought the sun and the flowers

Where there used to be rain'

Facilitating PTG

Among researchers and practitioners in the PTG area, there is a strong consensus that growth after adversity usually occurs quite organically. It is better to walk with the individual on their journey, rather than impose these ideas on someone. Perhaps notice growth experiences when they are vivid in someone's own thinking and actions (Calhoun & Tedeschi, 2013), rather than suggesting that growth is something that ought to happen. The following exercise is an invitation only – engage with it if you are interested in exploring it. I do want to emphasise that PTG is not something you must find or experience. It is completely normal to not connect with this theory or exercise.

—————————————— **ACTIVITY** ——————————————

Capturing transformative growth

In this exercise, I am building on the theory of PTG. I am also leaning on a meaning in life intervention devised by Steger and colleagues (2014). Here, we are aiming to recognise and appreciate post-traumatic growth in our lives. Choose one of the areas of PTG that naturally calls to you: Appreciation of life; Personal strength; Relating to others; New possibilities; Spiritual and existential change; or New awareness of the body.

1   Start taking photographs which reflect personal strength in your life after adversity.
2   Collect 8–12 photographs.
3   Collate the pictures together and ask yourself:
    a   What does this picture represent?
    b   How does the picture embody personal strength for you?
    c   If possible, write a little reflective note about each photo.

Note: If you have a visual impairment and are listening to this book as an audiobook, you could try this exercise by choosing a song that reflects one of the post-traumatic growth areas. Alternatively, select an object from your life that has this kind of tactile representation for you.

This exercise aims to help you notice the growth in your life; you can even use it to write yourself a new story from survivor to thriver (Calhoun & Tedeschi, 2013; Joseph, 2012). It is important to note that often distress and growth co-exist. This is natural. Sadness or grief does not disappear overnight, nor does it need to. Travel with kindness towards all that you feel.

Final thoughts

I want to thank you for taking this journey with me on this chapter. The topic area is challenging as well as powerful, with rays of hope within. In this last paragraph, I want to consider a lovely Japanese art tradition called the golden repair (*kintsugi* or *kintsukuroi*). If a beloved piece of pottery breaks, gold or other valued metals are used to repair the piece. The idea is that when something has suffered damage, this becomes part of its history. Rather than hiding its new features, we should celebrate them. I will finish this chapter with the words of a famous Finnish poet, Tommy Taberman, and suggest that '*Sometimes the most wholesome of us are made of smithereens*'.

Ten

Be playful

Robert Biswas-Diener

Introduction

My grandfather was the least playful person I have ever known. On a trip to Alaska, his travel journal was exclusively dedicated to recording the temperature and humidity, the high and low tides, and the times of sunrise and sunset. Another time, he snipped off the end of his pointer finger in a grain thresher and – according to family lore – finished his workday before seeking medical attention. After that, he always pointed with his middle finger and this made me laugh in the most imma-ture way possible. My grandfather never understood what I thought was so funny. He was smart, hardworking, loyal and generous. He was not, however, playful. I share the example of my grandfather only to suggest that there are many virtues and that not everyone has all of them. Playfulness is just one example. As a playful person myself, I recognise that joking and a fun-loving attitude can appear frivolous beside the more serious qualities of kindness, forgiveness and gratitude. Even so, I will make the case here that playfulness is as worthwhile as any of these.

Play permeates every aspect of society. We play games, we play sports, we play practical jokes, we play musical instruments and we attend plays. In English, we use the terms in a huge range of circumstances: 'play favourites', 'play hard-ball', 'play it by ear', 'play with fire', 'play dirty', 'play fair' and 'play hooky'. We set aside play*grounds* for children. In the United States, we have holidays, such as Halloween and April Fool's Day, that are centrally concerned with aspects of play. We even have historical examples of attention paid to play in the arts, sciences and philosophy. Hamlet, for example, said in Shakespeare's play of the same name, 'The play's the thing!' Albert Einstein famously said, 'God does not play dice with the universe.' Even Friedrich Nietzsche, known mostly for his pes-simistic view on the meaninglessness of life, said 'In every real man [sic] a child is hidden that wants to play.'

The purpose of this chapter is to give the concept of play central importance in the good life. By the conclusion of this chapter, you should be able to:

- define play
- articulate the differences between childhood play and adult play
- list three benefits of play
- identify at least one strategy for increasing play in your own life.

Playing by the rules: Defining play and its nature

We can see conspicuous examples of play in sports and in children pretending to travel to the moon. In fact, the wide-ranging instances of play can make it difficult to understand. Putting out a batsman in cricket and pretending to be in a starship seem fairly different from one another. And the sheer range of play only expands from there: video and board games, rough-housing, teasing, pretending, athletics, wordplay, comedy and parody, improvisation, betting, joking, or shoving your best friend into a swimming pool. Is there a common thread that connects the various types of play? Researchers suggest that they are all bound by the following characteristics (adapted from the work of Brown, 2009):

1 *Purposelessness*: play does not have to achieve a goal or make a meaningful impact.
2 *Voluntary*: play is the result of desire and people cannot be forced to play.
3 *Pleasurable*: play is inherently enjoyable.

To say that play is purposeless is not to dismiss its value. It merely refers to the idea that a game of tag or Monopoly, or a practical joke, are not primarily about achieving some desirable end. We don't need to trouble ourselves with pretending that we are improving society when we play soccer or play piano for our friends. Positive social impact or personal meaning do not need to be the reasons we are involved in board games or sports. Play doesn't need to have a lasting effect.

Even so, play can be beneficial. It is associated with healthy psychological development. This explains why it is universal: play is natural. One piece of evidence for this can be found in the fact that play is widely observed in animals, too. For example, play fighting and rough-housing have been documented in many species, including primates and pronghorn sheep (Miller & Byers, 1998). Researchers point to the play process in young, non-human animals as having evolutionary advantages, such as practising skills that will benefit them in maturity and preparing them for unexpected circumstances (Špinka et al., 2001).

We see similar behaviours in the tiny humans we call children. Most of us accept the idea that purposeless, enjoyable play is a natural part of being a child.

In fact, play appears critical to the social, emotional and cognitive development of children. Developmental psychologists have observed types of play in children emerging at various ages. For example, the 'solitary play' (playing alone) of very young children evolves into 'parallel play' (playing alongside but not interacting with others) and then into 'associative play' (interacting and sharing) and, finally, into 'cooperative play' (interacting to achieve a common objective) by about age 5 (Dyer & Moneta, 2006).

Much of childhood play is rooted in imagination. For example, children 'play house' in which they pretend to cook, put on make-up or mimic other adult activities. Although this type of play serves no immediate practical value – no food is actually prepared and no child really heads out for a night on the town – this form of play may have the psychological side-effect of allowing children to experiment with identities and to build skills (Sutton-Smith, 1997). Other forms of imaginative play, such as having an 'invisible friend', may serve as psychological benefits such as aiding problem-solving, providing comfort or as a mechanism for overcoming loneliness (Majors & Baines, 2017).

Interestingly, play is a largely cultural phenomenon, which dictates what we play and how we play. Adults living in the USA or the UK, for example, might reasonably play basketball or rugby, but they are almost certainly not playing *kabaddi* or *sepak takraw*, even though these sports are popular elsewhere. The influence of culture can especially be seen in how children play. Factors such as urbanisation, affluence and parents working outside the home all impact the ways that play is introduced to children. In traditional Yucatec Mayan society, for instance, childhood play is relatively discouraged in favour of enlisting kids into more productive activities that have a tangible benefit for the group (Gaskins et al., 2007), as in, 'Hey, you kids quit playing and give me a hand with this!' Even when children are allowed or encouraged to play, the play activity must fit with cultural worldviews and societal roles. Anecdotally, I witnessed this when conducting field research with traditional Maasai people, in Kenya. In the months I was with them, I never observed the children pretending to drive a racing car or fly a spaceship. I did, however, see them throwing rocks and sticks at imaginary animals. In another study, half the young children in a sample from the Dominican Republic reported having an invisible friend, whereas only 5% of children from a Nepali sample did so (Wigger, 2018). These cultural differences may reflect distinctions in societal emphases on imagination, fantasy proneness, religious views, and approaches to parenting.

Play is a concept less associated with adults than it is with children. In fact, only about 10% of all research on play examines this phenomenon in the adult context (van Leeuwen & Westwood, 2008). This makes conceptual sense because play is often thought of as a developmental process by which children prepare for adulthood. Even so, a casual look at the social lives of adults reveals many forms of play: social games, sexual role-play, gambling, athletics, video games, and telling jokes, to name a few. Although adult play is defined by the hallmarks of purposelessness and enjoyment, it differs from childhood play in its relative structure. You will note that in the previous examples, there is a relatively high degree of structure to the play; rules are followed and there is a clear objective within the play. In most societies, adults are discouraged from socially engaging in structureless play, especially pretend or silliness. As a result, the majority of adults develop inhibitions against such play, and this can easily be seen in many people's adverse reactions to being invited to participate in improvisational theatre games. In fact, adults who lack such inhibitions (those who come across as highly playful: being silly, funny, imaginative and entertaining) are often viewed as having a playful personality (Proyer & Ruch, 2011). That is, they are seen as a unique minority where play is concerned.

The play's the thing: The benefits of play

Research reveals that engaging in play and play-like activities is widely beneficial. For example, the character strength of humour (arguably related to play) appears to be associated with wellbeing and negatively correlated with depressive symptoms (Gander et al., 2019). Humour isn't just about asking, 'Why did the toilet paper roll down the hill?', it is also about teasing, improvising and wordplay. In essence, it is a playful mindset. Perhaps this is the reason that humour seems to be one of the qualities most strongly predictive of wellbeing across the lifespan (Martínez-Martí & Ruch, 2014). Humorous people may be more likely to connect with others, make a game out of small hardships, or see the funny side of life.

Similarly, the concept of leisure (also, arguably, related to play) is associated with higher rates of happiness (Lu & Argyle, 1994). That's right; even though work can be meaningful, carefree downtime makes for an enjoyable life. You can see this in your own life: too much study, intellectual discussion and part-time work feel more manageable if paired with the occasional board game or volleyball match. In fact, too little play can be downright unhealthy. Brown (2014) warns of the concept of 'play deprivation' in childhood. He reports that mild or moderate deficiencies in play are associated with more defensiveness, difficulties with long-term intimacy, and other interpersonal challenges. For those who experience severe play deprivation, the consequences are more profound: the development of fewer prosocial behaviours such as cooperation and altruism, and a negative effect on the ability to manage emotional responses in a healthy way.

It is due to the benefits of play that I believe we can treat this concept as important (but not serious!). The research literature from happiness specifically, and positive psychology more broadly, tends to place an emphasis on virtuous activity (Ryan et al., 2013; Vittersø, 2013). As a result, researchers and practitioners in this field sometimes run the risk of minimising the importance of activities that are primarily pleasurable (Ryan & Deci, 2001; Ryff, 1989; Waterman, 1993). Forgiveness and charitable giving, for instance, can easily be treated as more worthwhile pursuits than playing cards with one's friends or making a sandcastle at the beach. I argue that climbing a tree, playing a game of charades and telling jokes are important pastimes.

Despite its apparent lack of purpose, play confers a wide range of psychological benefits that add value to the concept. Here, I will review just two of the benefits of play that have received research attention – flow and restoration.

Flow

Flow, also known as 'being in the zone', is characterised by a loss of the sense of self, losing track of time, and is remembered as highly enjoyable (Csikszentmihalyi, 2008). It is no accident that Csikszentmihalyi, the researcher who pioneered this field of study, is an avid rock-climber and chess player. Activities that are inherently enjoyable and which focus attention away from the self and onto the activity are more likely to produce flow experiences. This includes play, broadly defined. For instance, playing a musical instrument, engaging in recreational sex, playing games of chance, performing as an athlete or even as a mimic are considered flow activities (Csikszentmihalyi, 2008). Flow might serve an important function for motivation and the development of certain skills; a process that might otherwise be frustrating, discouraging or experienced as negative (Vittersø, 2011).

Restoration

Play is restorative. That is, it appears to restore the homeostatic balance within a person. What!?! Homeostatic balance? That has to be one of the least playful phrases in the English language! It simply means that engaging in play can restore a person's attention and emotion (Vittersø, 2011). Evidence for this comes from studies of video-game players (Rupp et al., 2017) who report improved mood and focus after casual game play. In another study, playfulness was associated with higher levels of emotional support, coping, positive reframing, and humour among hundreds of university students (Magnuson & Barnett, 2013). There are many reasons why playfulness might be linked to psychological restoration, including the possibility that playful people cope better, that it is possible to buffer against stress with the enjoyment of play, and that many forms of play include supportive companionship (Qian & Yarnal, 2011). Interestingly, the context of play matters for restoration: distractions such as noise that can potentially interfere with focused attention can lead to diminished restoration in the form of a less positive mood state (Vitterso et al., 2004).

Playing: Hard to get

So, being playful is natural. Not only is it enjoyable, play is good for you. It is a wonder, then, that we spend so little time doing it. A variety of time-use survey studies paint an interesting portrait of the ways that people spend a typical day. For example, in a recent United Nations development report (UNDP, 2015) socialising and leisure account for approximately 15–20% of daily activity worldwide. Although this typically translates to at least two full hours of leisure time each day, this time does not always present itself as a monolithic block. Thus, it may be important for people to prioritise playfulness by scheduling it. You can also make time for play by appreciating that humour, teasing and wordplay can be done in very short bursts of time and can be threaded into other activities, including work.

Another potential obstacle to daily play is the effort it takes. It is possible that more time-demanding playful pastimes feel more effortful. This might explain why people are likely to engage in passive pursuits such as watching television when they find they have free time. After a long study session or a stressful shift at work, people often want to relax. It is certainly easier and more convenient to open a social media app than it is to change clothes and meet your friends at a nearby park for an impromptu game. It is here that many people forget about the benefits of play. Meeting your friends might seem like a burden, but it is also likely to feel restorative, fun and connecting. Remembering the play paradox – the fact that effort and focus can be restorative – can be helpful in inserting more play into your life.

A review of your own leisure time use will reveal a fair amount of physically and mentally passive activities: television and film viewing and social media use being the primary examples. These may be enjoyable and voluntary activities, but they are less associated with playfulness. In fact, heavy television viewing is associated with lower mood (Kubey & Csikszentmihalyi, 1990). It may be that screen time replaces more physically active and playful pursuits, and that those who engage in excessive and passive screen time do not gain the benefits of play.

Final thoughts

You don't have to be a stand-up comedian, a professional athlete, a jazz musician or a child to enjoy play. True, there are people with playful personalities, but all of us can enjoy a joke or a game. More than anything, you need to make time for play and remember that play – unlike some work – is restorative, even if it initially seems effortful. You already engage in make-believe in the privacy of your own fantasies. You almost certainly enjoy some form of game-playing. To some degree, you have a sense of humour, even if it is just the appreciation of other people's jokes. Now, keep in mind that these playful qualities are important and beneficial. Play is undeniably part of the good life.

ACTIVITY

Learning how to be more playful

1 Recognise that play is legitimate. Do not dismiss it as being frivolous or childish. Instead, embrace play as a highly beneficial part of the good life.

2 Experiment with play. There are structured types of play such as games and sports that have clear rules. There are improvisational types of play like joking. There are creative forms of play like painting for fun or making a collage. Allow yourself to try a variety of types of play so that you can better learn what you enjoy and what restores you.

3 Consider the effort paradox – that is, many types of play such as board games and athletics seem more effortful than do watching TV or scrolling through social media. Even so, active play is far more restorative for your mood and attention than are those common and passive pastimes. The effort is worth it!

Eleven
Find meaning

Michael Steger

Introduction

I am a Generation Xer, but not one of the 'put the time in, climb the corporate ladder, retire with a pension' believers. I was a cynical Generation Xer, and when I was at university, I was already feeling disillusioned by the poisoning of nature, entrenched injustice, the death of family farms, the abandonment of factories and manufacturing workforces, and the pillaging of pension funds. I already had no faith that there would be any social safety net that would catch me and my generation when we got sick or dared to retire. And I was already certain that the Baby Boomers would soak the world dry, fill it with pollution, run the government coffers down to empty, and circle their Porsches and Ferraris within their gated communities while the rest of us ate rats.

You now have enough information to make accurate guesses about how much fun I was at parties and you can also judge for yourself if I was prophetic, deluded or just spouting the anti-establishment creed of my day. The point here is that however unreliable and haphazard the world looked to my eyes back then, you, as university students today, are facing a chaotic and stressful world of your own, and it's OK (at least to me) if it all seems like madness to you. It's like the world is seen through a pulsating kaleidoscope where disasters and miracle technology, injustice and humanitarianism, hope and fear all whirl around faster and faster. Under those kinds of conditions, we tend to worry about what we can count on, what the future holds or how much effort it is worth putting towards our goals or dreams. At the same time, for some of you, the world might still look like it is just waiting to give you an incredible life of adventure, exploration, travel, warm relationships and a carousel of airport lounges and infinity pools. Whether to your eyes the world looks like a family-friendly version of *Mad Max* or a lifestyle influencer's dream come true, there is one universal desire that we all come face to face with eventually: we want our lives to be meaningful.

This chapter will share with you some of the main findings that 'meaning in life' researchers like myself have uncovered and some of the best strategies for finding, enhancing and using meaning to deal with stress, build psychological resilience and create a life that is worth living.

In this chapter, you will:

- demystify the idea of meaning in life and learn three user-friendly approaches
- uncover the broad and deep impact that meaning has in our lives
- capture and nurture the wellsprings of meaning in your life right now
- learn strategies to actively and intentionally live meaning – each day.

Making meaning easier to understand

Meaning and purpose seem incredibly popular right now. Actors, business leaders, coaches and athletes, politicians and charity leaders, teachers, doctors, nurses and so many other people are now sharing their struggles and triumphs and telling us how they found meaning and purpose in their lives. When they talk about meaning and purpose, they seem to be trying to express the feelings or beliefs that are most important to them, or the reasons why it is worth continuing to strive, or sometimes they are just talking about gaining some new perspective on all the craziness they are seeing. Sometimes they are talking about a profound sense of motivation or a feeling of deep fulfillment or contentment. Sometimes they seem to be saying that they have a direction for their lives or have connected with some vast or sacred truth. I could go on. There are so many ways that people talk about meaning – everything from dumping a toxic friend to finding new music to feeling like the whole universe suddenly makes sense. Each of these different topics expresses a little part of what meaning in life is all about.

'In' not 'of'

To get a better idea of what we are talking about, let's start with what we are *not* talking about. We are not talking about The Meaning *of* Life. Instead, we are talking about meaning *in* life. Think about that difference. The Meaning of Life suggests that we have to be incredibly wise or faithful to be confident that we have everything in the universe, from creation to death, all figured out. When we shift to looking at meaning *in* life, we are really talking about the journey each unique person takes through their lifetime, in the world they encounter, in the way they see things. Unlike The Meaning of Life, meaning *in* life helps us see that there is no single, absolute answer. Rather, there are many little answers that keep us leaning towards a better life for ourselves and the world we learn to love.

One of the great things about psychology research is that we can take huge concepts like meaning and both bring an orderly system to them (i.e. build theory) and quantify the consequences of when they are present in people's lives (i.e. measure and get data). We will look at both of these ways that research helps us, beginning with the theory behind meaning in life.

From a theoretical perspective, it is a deep and extremely human need to want life to have meaning (Frankl, 1963). Because we are able to think about our lives abstractly, we seek to put it all in order and find a niche for ourselves in the grand scheme of things. Without it, we can lose hope, motivation, joy, our sense of the special-ness of human life or even the will to live. But we do not have to figure *everything* out, just our own stuff. Meaning in life scholars agree that meaning in life is a positive psychological judgement about one's own life. We do not put any particular requirements on what people have to think about when we ask them if their lives are meaningful. In fact, they are able to use whatever subjective standards they would like (Steger et al., 2006). Because of this, it is certainly possible that people could be 'wrong' about whether their lives truly are meaningful (they might be shallow, for example), but it is not clear who should get to decide the objective meaningfulness of everyone's lives. What is interesting about this approach is that whether people are right or wrong in some objective sense, there are many similarities in the kinds of information and experiences people think about when they are judging meaning in their own lives. Three main themes emerge, in fact, which researchers call the three dimensions of meaning in life (e.g. Martela & Steger, 2016). These three dimensions are:

- *Coherence*, which is about how people make sense of their lives and come to understand the degree to which life is consistent and predictable – coherence captures the 'rules' we think run the world behind the scenes, whether those rules are supported by science (e.g. 'good people live longer lives', which is generally supported) or not (e.g. 'the lizardmen Illuminati faked the moon landing to hide the truth that the earth is flat', which is not true).
- *Purpose*, which is about the kinds of aspirations and dreams people want to achieve in their lives, and the way that they use those aspirations to motivate themselves, make decisions and set their priorities in life.
- *Significance*, which is about the strength of our beliefs that our own life has inherent value, that it is worth living even during hard times and that who we are and what we do matter in some sense – Viktor Frankl, who survived four different concentration camps during the Second World

War and lost almost all of his family during the Holocaust, argued that even when everything else has been taken away from us, we still have the ability to choose how we will endure our suffering, which in turn can serve as an example and encouragement to others (Frankl, 1963). Thus, even in the worst of times, it is worth living meaningfully because our example matters to others.

What research tells us about meaning

Researchers need data, which means that we cannot study something like the true meaning of the universe, why there is death or whether there is a reason for everything that has happened over the past trillion years or so. You cannot ask the universe why it was created. Instead, we study the individual experience of each person as they work to create meaning in their lives. Taking each of those individual paths and aggregating them together with others, we build databases of people at all positions in that journey – from those in despair to those leading inspiringly meaningful lives. Then we can pick our patterns and test their strength and statistical significance. One significant pattern has emerged from research time and time again: people who see their lives as meaningful are better off in just about every way conceivable.

─────────── POINTS FOR REFLECTION ───────────

Meaning and living a good life

What is fascinating about this large and rapidly growing body of research is that it essentially does not matter where in the world you do the research or what you use as your outcomes, meaning in life is one of the very small number of irrefutably vital parts of living a happy, good life:

- *Meaning in life is linked to our personal experience of wellbeing.* Hundreds of research studies have shown that high levels of meaning in life correlate or even predict people's feelings of happiness, joy, vitality, energy, optimism, contentment, and quality and satisfaction of life (e.g. Chamberlain & Zika, 1988; Edwards & van Tongeren, 2020; Shek, 1995; Steger & Frazier, 2005; Steger et al., 2006, 2008a, 2008b).
- *Meaning in life is linked to positive feelings about ourselves, and our relationships with others.* Another major area of research has focused on the role that meaning in life plays in supporting self-esteem, self-worth, self-acceptance and authenticity (e.g. Steger et al., 2008c). People with high levels of meaning in life feel more confident and authentic in who they are and are able to translate

that into better, more loving relationships (Ryff, 1989; Shek, 1995). They more often experience love, they are closer to other people, they are better listeners and friends, their marriages are more satisfying, and they are more satisfied with their sex lives (McCann & Biaggio, 1989; Steger et al., 2008a; Stillman et al., 2011). Other people notice something magnetic about these people, and in lab experiments, they rate people high in meaning to be more enjoyable, express a stronger interest in interacting with them again, and even think they would be better candidates for future friendships (Lambert et al., 2013).

- *Meaning in life is linked to better coping with stress and adversity.* People with high levels of meaning in life feel less stressed out, their bodies have lower levels of stress indicators, they use more effective coping techniques, and they are significantly more likely to see ways in which they have grown as a person after living through adversity or trauma (e.g. Jim et al., 2006; Steger et al., 2008d, 2015).

- *Meaning in life is linked to better health.* People with high levels of meaning in life feel healthier and *are* physically healthier across a wide range of biomarkers (e.g. Krause & Hayward, 2012; Roepke et al., 2014; Steger et al., 2015). This may be due to the fact that they engage in healthier lifestyles: better nutrition and diet, more physical activity, less substance misuse, a greater willingness to use prophylactics to avoid sexually transmitted infections, and better use of preventative care (e.g. Brassai et al., 2015; Kim et al., 2014; Piko & Brassai, 2009; Steger et al., 2015).

- *A meaningful life is a longer life.* Numerous studies have shown that high levels of meaning in life can predict how long people will live many years later, even after controlling for other well-known factors that can shorten people's lives, such as income, depression, disability, chronic medical conditions, and more (see Cohen et al., 2016, for a meta-analysis of a dozen such studies).

So, meaning in life leads to happier, longer, better lives for yourself and others. What's not to like? Well, there's everything to like, actually, which sometimes puts pressure on people to think that they have to have everything figured out already and have fierce convictions about their ironclad meaning in life. If your vision of meaning in life does not seem that clear, don't worry! There is one additional angle on meaning that is especially relevant to you as university students. So far, we have talked about how people experience meaning in life; how they would rate their lives from very meaningless to extremely meaningful. Researchers have also explored people's different tendencies to search for meaning. That is, regardless of how much you experience meaning in your life, you might be more or less engaged in a process of questioning and searching for meaning. Young people are more likely than older folk to be searching for meaning, which indicates that it is very normal to have more questions than answers at that stage (Steger et al., 2008b). So, if you do not have it all figured out yet, that is normal. It is OK. To help you feel more comfortable in your search for meaning, the next section of this chapter will give you some activities you can try and some questions to ask yourself that research shows help many people find more meaning in life.

Putting meaning into action

Before we rush into the steps you can take to gain clarity on meaning in your life and how to infuse everyday life with purpose, it is important to reiterate that a big part of meaning in life is exploration and being comfortable with not quite knowing enough yet. There seems to be a hidden assumption many of us hold about ourselves that we are 'a thing' and our job is to get to know about our thing and then get on with making a life with it. We are supposed to be certain about who we are, what we want, what is best for us and where we are going, which leads to a lot of pressure to find our meaning and purpose. There is not much evidence that such ideas hold merit. But, even if you are absolutely convinced that you are going to be the same easy-to-figure-out 'thing' your whole life, no matter what happens, for just this moment, try to adopt the perspective that you will change, evolve and adapt over the years and experiences, that there are contradictions in you and even that you have competing impulses – some of which lead you to virtue and some to vice – that might never stop bickering for your attention. Rather than viewing yourself as something like a non-player character (NPC) that can be described and pinned down in a few words and idiosyncrasies, view yourself as the open-ended world you are there to explore. There will be both surprises and long periods of slogging along, both helpers and opponents, dangerous terrain and places of rest and regeneration, and through your adventuring you will learn what works and what fails, where it is useful to go and where you hit dead ends or worse. This perspective of approaching your life and self as a journey rather than as 'a thing' is potentially so important that it is the first suggestion for putting meaning into action.

--------------------- ACTIVITY ---------------------

Enjoying the journey

Each day for a week, decide that you will take an hour to try on the perspective that understanding who you are and what you want from life is an adventure to explore, not just a destination to tick off your list. For each decision, situation and experience during that hour, try to pay attention to how you respond and how you make decisions about what to do next. What do you learn from your initial instincts? How do you talk to yourself as you choose? How do you encode events through your self-talk? The overarching question is *What do you learn about yourself through curiosity and paying attention?*

Doing the exploration activity might feel a little bizarre because we are more used to watching ourselves to correct what we do or avoid mistakes than we are to learn. However, other than the laws of physics, *you* are the one constant in your life, so it is worth it to learn more. The below nostalgia activity is another one that helps you learn more about yourself that is easy and backed by research as a way of bringing more meaning into your life (Routledge et al., 2011).

ACTIVITY

Being nostalgic

Living in the past is not a good idea but visiting every once in a while is an excellent way to learn about what and who matters to us and how we have changed over time. It also helps us to develop tools for how to craft and shape our life stories. Set aside at least three separate hours in a week when you can take a trip down memory lane. You can look at old photos or posts, read your journals, start thinking about your school friends, teachers or teams/clubs (really just about anything), and your goal is to focus on special and important memories.

From a focus on the past, we pivot to a focus on the future and developing awareness of purpose. Your life is probably filled with goals, assignments and due dates. So many of these are set for us that our goals might feel like insignificant tweaks of a programme someone else created. Purpose is about finding and working towards a dream or an aspiration truly worth striving for ... for you. We will start small and learn as we go.

ACTIVITY

Moving from values to action

Today, you will pick a different kind of goal. First, spend a moment thinking about and writing down your values. To help them clarify their values, I like to ask people 'What do you stand for?' and 'What would you *never* stand for?' That is, what values do you want to represent in the world, and what kinds of actions would you either resist or shun? However large of a list you create, pick one of them and set a goal to engage in one visible action that supports that value each day for a week. That is, you are creating a goal to turn your values into action for a week.

As your understanding of yourself and what you stand for grows, you will be doing more and more each day that is meaningful. From a meaning perspective, it is also important that our journey through life is not only about us, but embraces people, life and the world around us as well. This expansion of our concerns is called self-transcendence. Self-transcendence is key to building deep meaning and purpose in our lives and helps us know that our lives are significant.

ACTIVITY

Learning from your role models

Let's start with role models. Who or what inspires you? It can be a family member, a famous historical figure or even a song or work of art. Spend some time identifying your inspirations. When you have found a handful or so, ask yourself why they inspire you. What goals did they have? What impact? What qualities? If you have heard of them and are inspired by them, they must have made an impact beyond their own lives, so how did their influence make it all the way to you?

The inspiration activity gets us looking at how other people have transcended their selves in some way. And if they can do it, we can too.

ACTIVITY

Pushing yourself further

Many people say they want to make the world a better place. That is wonderful, but a bit vague. Take an hour or so to get specific about how you can live your life to make things better for something that is outside of yourself and your personal life. What parts of the world do you want to make better? Do you care about nature, refugees, preserving history and culture, justice, freedom, education, curing sickness, comforting the lonely, or other important things? Try as hard as you can to create a ranked list of these causes that you care about. Then take a look at the top couple of picks and identify one change you can make to your routine in the next week that would make a positive difference to that cause. Try to push yourself a little bit beyond making a donation or signing a pledge and think about how your everyday activities could be modified to make a difference. In other words, embed a little self-transcendence in your everyday life.

There is a lot of thinking and writing and planning in these activities so far, so the final suggestion, photojournalism, is slightly easier and a bit different.

ACTIVITY

Dabbling in photojournalism

Each day for the next week, take one photo that answers the question 'What makes your life meaningful?' It is important to space the photos out each day to let subtle or even hidden sources of meaning emerge. You can take photos of people, places, objects and symbols. For example, if you cannot be near a person or place that makes your life meaningful, you can take a photo of a symbol, even another photo. At the end of the week, you can post each photo or chat with a friend or loved one, making sure to describe why each one is meaningful to you.

Final thoughts

The hope of this chapter is that no matter how chaotic and uncertain the world might seem to you right now, there are perspectives you can learn and things you can do each day that can help you build meaning, both as a resource for coping with all the madness and as a key element to what makes life good and well worth living. The activity suggestions provided in this chapter are specific to meaning, but there are many other activities you can do that indirectly boost meaning, such as engaging in acts of kindness, having an intimate and fearless conversation with a close friend or family member, helping another person celebrate a success, practising being grateful for any good that happens in your life, and cultivating mindfulness. The truth is that there are many paths we each can travel to nurture and cultivate meaning in life. Those paths exist and are there for us to discover, whether the world looks safe or scary.

Twelve

Learn about yourself

Aaron Jarden and Rebecca Jarden

Introduction

You now have knowledge and insights into a range of wellbeing topics. The purpose of this chapter is to help you understand how you can use this understanding to embed your learning. You can think of this as the supercharger chapter!

First, we'll think of ourselves as scientists and then explore the importance of learning through trial and error – what some call 'positive failure'. Following this, we outline a way of creating tiny habits, and introduce two strategies that are critical to your wellbeing in a university context: slowing down and making life simple. We then move beyond the individual to a broader systemic framework by considering how the concept of *Me, We, Us*, can help with self-care and wellbeing initiatives. Finally, we discuss wider systems of support (e.g. friends, family) that can aid you in your wellbeing.

In this chapter, we will explore:

- the importance of self-experimentation and positive failure
- a wellbeing assessment which will provide information about your wellbeing and self-care
- a behaviour change framework and a habit formation process
- the 'Me, We, Us' framework to understand how systems impact your wellbeing and self-care.

Being your own scientist

In this chapter, we are encouraging you to see yourself as a scientist, using the principles and practices of science to experiment on yourself. Or, as we would put it, when reporting a scientific result, you are 'N = 1' – where the 'N' in scientific notation refers to the full sample size, the total population – and that population sample size in this instance is you! Such individualised experimental approaches have been common across many of the social sciences, including applied positive psychology (Linley & Joseph, 2004), clinical psychology (Kramer et al., 2013), counselling psychology (Gelso et al., 2014) and coaching psychology (Passmore & Theeboom, 2016). Wellbeing is highly individual. That is why this experimental approach is particularly relevant. It honours the principle that 'you are the expert of you' and so the positive psychological interventions (PPIs: Parks & Schueller, 2014) – or, as we call them, 'wellbeing-enhancing activities' – that you choose to engage with should be based on what you think will work best for you.

Underpinning your experimentation is the 'scientist-practitioner' approach (Peterson & Park, 2005). The scientist-practitioner model has been around for many years and encourages a mutually informing relationship between research and practice. When you experiment, you should allow your practice to be informed by the research literature, while learning which activities and strategies work for you. Maybe you have found an affinity with 'strengths use' (see Chapter 3), but think being more 'hopeful' (see Chapter 4) is not that useful for you. Maybe you appreciate the value of positive 'relationships' (see Chapter 8), but find thinking about 'adversity' is not that helpful for you (see Chapter 9). The reality is that some of these strategies will work for you, some will not, some will work a little bit, and some will take a while to work. One of the ways to find out is to experiment and give them a go, but there is a strategic way to go about doing this.

Positive failure

No one enjoys failing, but it turns out that some people benefit from doing so (Arnott, 2013). Every failure offers constructive lessons about oneself. Failure itself is a natural and powerful psychological force, yet it can be treated as a taboo topic in some social circles. It would be unusual to introduce yourself to new people at a social event with a line about how you failed a first-year academic subject! However, there is a notion of 'positive failure' which is defined as 'a failure after appropriate investment that leads to further learning or development' (Arnott, 2013, p. 4). From this perspective, a dose of failure is like being vaccinated – while not initially pleasant, it can be good over the longer term because trying and failing can lead to development and growth. And it is in this sense that a dose of failure can be embraced – through a focus on the learning that comes from the experience and doing things differently next time.

It is important to understand that learning involves being out of your comfort zone. Experiences of frustration, while unpleasant, are actually markers that you are on a positive learning growth curve. Positive failure is about setting up a process where you keep learning and trying until you achieve your goals. There may even be situations where early successes might not be good for you! The way you embrace the learning that comes from failure can be a superpower over the long term. So, how do you know if your experiments are succeeding or not? To answer that, let's explore another aspect of being a scientist – the topic of wellbeing assessment.

Wellbeing assessment

Assessment and tracking will help determine your levels of psychological wellbeing at any one point in time. Even better, it will help to identify which wellbeing interventions could be of most help to you. This vital information can help you understand what aspects of your current lifestyle are working for you. Without it, you are effectively flying blind. Your own wellbeing assessments provide you with a data source that you can use to select wellbeing activities to include in your experiments.

There are two stages to 'assessing' wellbeing. First, we need to collect information. This is usually done through a survey or test, often online. Second, we need to look over the results of the survey or test and make an evaluation about what it is telling us. But what do wellbeing assessments measure? As you have seen in this book, there are numerous definitions of wellbeing but overall it is generally accepted that wellbeing incorporates aspects of what is going well in life as well as aspects of illbeing (having depressed mood, feeling lonely, experiencing stress, etc.). In this way, wellbeing is understood as a continuum. A balanced life comprises both positive and negative experiences. Therefore, a wellbeing assessment ought to capture both what is going well and what is not going so well. Often, it does this by evaluating aspects of emotions (e.g. happiness, joy), thoughts (e.g. life satisfaction judgements), behaviours (e.g. movement, thankfulness in relationships) and sometimes physiology (e.g. heart rate variability).

Whatever particular wellbeing assessment you decide on, it is important to take regular assessments over time so that you can assess any changes and reflect on the findings. For example, if you are working on becoming more mindful and assessing mindfulness over time, you can gauge the extent to which your level of mindfulness is increasing. If you find that your mindfulness is not increasing, then either the activities you are undertaking are not effective for you or, alternatively, the assessment measure that assesses mindfulness might not be a good one. This approach supports setting growth targets and aspirations for your wellbeing going forward. Think of this a bit like going to the doctor for a regular medical check-up. In this case, it is about your mental health. This insight could set you apart from the pack, help you take proactive action if needed, and be the foundation for your wellbeing and performance. At the end of this chapter, we recommend some short and easy-to-use resources to begin this wellbeing assessment practice.

Behaviour change and habits

So, let's imagine that you are on board with the idea of self-experimentation and that you have some wellbeing assessments in place. What's next? Well, you now have the raw ingredients to put together your own personalised wellbeing plan. Below, we're going to help you do that as effectively as possible, using the latest research in behaviour change. What is needed to change a behaviour? The work of B. J. Fogg (2020), from the Stanford Behavior Change Institute, suggests that three things need to happen at the same time for a behaviour to occur. He summarises this in the following formula:

B = MAP where B is behaviour, M is motivation, A is ability and P is prompt

A behaviour happens when you are motivated to do it, you have the ability and you are prompted to put that ability into action. Motivation comes from wanting to achieve pleasure, be accepted and attain hopes, or from avoiding pain, fear and rejection. Abilities include things such as time, money, physical and mental capacity, and social support. Prompts are things such as reminders, calls to action, sparks, facilitators, or other kinds of triggers in your life. Fogg's research suggests that these three ingredients – motivation, ability and prompt – need to happen simultaneously in order for a behaviour to occur, and if any one of these is missing, the behaviour is less likely to be forthcoming.

Fogg (2020) also studied the most effective ways to change a behaviour. His advice is to forget about big change and instead start with a 'tiny habit', making sure that you celebrate after you do the behaviour so that you are motivated to repeat it again and again (see Chapter 5). In designing for the new behaviour, Fogg recommends using an existing behaviour as an anchor and putting the new tiny behaviour after it, so that the old behaviour is the prompt for the new behaviour – and then designing a celebration that will help you be motivated to do it again the next time the prompt occurs. So you end up with A (anchor), B (behaviour) and C (celebration). The method is an 'after/then/I will' statement, such as 'After I … (existing behaviour), then I will … (new tiny habit) and

I will … (to celebrate)'. For example, after I brush my teeth, then I take one deep mindful breath and I will celebrate by smiling at myself in the mirror. The aim is to increase the tiny habit over time as it becomes more automated. Let's now turn to applying this to two strategies we see as critical to your wellbeing in a university context – slowing down and simplifying life.

Slowing down and simplifying life

Based on over 20 years of experience as university lecturers and academic research, we believe that these two strategies – slowing down and simplifying – are central to increasing wellbeing, greater self-care and improved academic performance in a university environment. This is because both counterbalance the 'VUCA' world we currently live in. VUCA is an acronym, first used in 1985 (Bennis & Nanus, 1985), to describe the Volatility, Uncertainty, Complexity and Ambiguity of general conditions and situations. It is with this backdrop that we have selected these two strategies, slowing down and simplifying, as key to enabling your self-care and wellbeing in the university environment.

Slowing down

There is a famous seven-page letter written by Harry Lewis, a professor at Harvard University, called 'Slow down: Getting more out of Harvard by doing less' (Lewis, 2004). In the letter, Lewis encourages new students at Harvard to essentially slow down, do less and not take on too many challenges. The letter speaks about the need for students to enjoy their time at Harvard, spending less free time in the many extracurricular activities, and to spend more unstructured time being absorbed with friends and doing what they love. Lewis writes: 'you are more likely to sustain the intense effort needed to accomplish first-rate work in one area if you allow yourself some leisure time, some recreation, some time for solitude, rather than packing your schedule with so many activities that you have no time to think about why you are doing what you are doing' (2004, p. 2). The essential idea of the letter is to spend more of your time on a few things you discover you truly love; to slow down and absorb yourself in these things.

While many areas of life are speeding up and we are being encouraged to do more in less time, we are now seeing a counter-movement. From speed yoga to fast food and speed dating, we are now starting to be interested in slow food, slow cities, slow sex and slow work. Studies have linked slowness to increased happiness, health and productivity (Honoré, 2004). There is a growing realisation that in order to reach one's human potential and excellence, a person needs downtime in order to recuperate energy and avoid burnout.

Here are three things you can do:

- *Take three deep breaths*. When you breathe out the first time, relax your physical body on the exhale. When you breathe out on the second exhale, think of what you are grateful for *right now*. Say to yourself, 'Right now, I am grateful for X'. On the third exhale out, put your mind into the intentional state you want it to be in – for example, being open-minded or curious. Say to yourself, 'My intention right now is to be… (kind, open-minded, relaxed, critical, curious, etc.)'.
- *Turn off all your devices and screens more often*. This will make you slow down and encourage you to connect with others for relationship benefits.
- *Whatever you do, do it slowly*. For example, walk that little bit slower to absorb and savour more of your environment.

Let's apply the tiny habits design principles to slowing down: Motivation + Ability + Prompt. Do you have the motivation to slow down? Can you see how it would benefit your energy, stress levels and performance? Do you have the ability to slow down? What prompts could you use to help you slow down? And what could a new tiny habit look like in action? What could your A (anchor), B (behaviour) and C (celebration) be? For example, imagine that you are motivated and able to slow down, and feel that you would benefit from slowing down with regard to social engagements at university. Your ABC might be: 'After I complete a university class, I will slow down by taking three deep breaths before getting up and engaging with friends'. Another one might be: 'After I complete a university lecture, I will go for a 3-minute walk by myself before meeting up with friends'.

Simplifying life

Simplifying has been regularly defined and cited as 'paring down to the essentials of life, what is important to you' (Mazza, 1997, p. 12). A typical dictionary definition is: 'to make less complex or complicated; make plainer or easier' (dictionary. com). We define simplifying as making something less complicated through two components: (1) an aspect of *doing less* (in quantity) – for instance, reducing your to-do list from eight things to five; and (2) an aspect of *prioritising* (in quality) – such as ordering those five things left on the to-do list by importance.

Whereas all the wellbeing and self-care activities in this book are in essence adding to your life (they are asking you to do more, be more), the idea of simplifying is asking you to do less, but to do less of the least important things. We want you to think about and cut away some of the clutter in your life to make room for things that are more important and more energising. You may also have to be proactive and say 'no' more. In many ways, what you say 'no' to can be more important than what you say 'yes' to.

Here are three things you can do:

- *Aim to do less* when faced with choices and options. For example, would you like to join the volleyball club *and* write a section for the university magazine *and* be the class representative? There are only so many hours in a day. Consider your strengths and passions and choose the option that is best for you, rather than all three. One of the most important things you need to master is the capacity to make choices that are appropriate to you, and slowing down is a pathway to this.
- *Prioritise* what is most important to you. As in the above example, if the student chooses to write for the university magazine and not participate in volleyball or to be the class representative, this is what was deemed most important to them. Only by knowing and having insight into your values (Chapter 3), having a sense of meaning and purpose in life (Chapter 11), and having insight into your strengths (Chapter 3) can you strategically prioritise what is most important to you before opting to do less.
- *Consider using 'tiny habits'* to move in this direction. Imagine you were motivated to simplify. Your ABC might be: 'After I plan out my academic study week (anchor), I will simplify by making a to-do list of all possible engagements and prioritise it (behaviour) before I get a cup of coffee (celebration)'. Another one might be: 'After I plan out my academic study week (anchor), I will simplify by choosing to do less of my prioritised to-do list and focusing on the things at the top of the list (behaviour) and I will savour the sense of achievement in doing that (celebration)'.

Until this point, we have focused on what you can do individually to bring your personalised wellbeing plan to life. However, it is also pertinent to think about systems beyond yourself and particularly how your self-care activities and initiatives fit into wider systems of support that can also impact on your wellbeing. Therefore, before we cover some of these systems, we demonstrate how a simple and handy framework, 'Me, We, Us', can help your thinking about systems and processes of change.

The 'Me, We, Us' framework

There is a new developing field within positive psychology called 'systems-informed positive psychology' (Kern et al., 2020), which 'explicitly incorporates principles and approaches from the systems sciences into positive psychology theory, methodologies, practices and discourse to optimise human social systems and the individuals within them' (p. 705). Within this 'systems-informed' backdrop, wellbeing assessments and activities can happen at three distinct levels of a system: the individual level (Me; a student, a lecturer, an administrator), the group level (We; pairs of students, student and lecturer, student and administrator) and the organisational level (Us; the university), as depicted in the 'Me, We, Us' framework (Jarden & Jarden, 2016) in Figure 12.1.

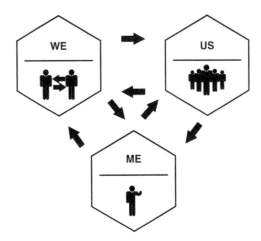

Figure 12.1   Me, We and Us levels of wellbeing in a system

- 'Me' level wellbeing activities include strategies and tasks that we can do by ourselves, such as learning about and utilising our strengths mindfully or undertaking a mindfulness programme (Niemiec, 2013), or slowing down (Honoré, 2004) and simplifying (Alexander & Ussher, 2012).
- 'We' level wellbeing activities involve work on our wellbeing that can be undertaken in a one-to-one or group format. These activities cannot be undertaken by individuals themselves as they require cooperation and input from others. For example, for students this may be with their lecturers, other university staff (e.g. guidance counsellors) or classmates, and can include strategies and tasks such as building 'high quality connections' (Dutton & Heaphy, 2003) or delivering gratitude letters to favourite lecturers (Norrish, 2015).
- Organisational and whole-of-university wellbeing initiatives include strategies and tasks that aim to have an impact on the whole community. Examples of 'Us' activities for universities include strategies and tasks such as creating a university wellbeing policy (HAPIA, 2009), directing resources towards one-off wellbeing initiatives, or whole-of-university wellbeing programs such as Appreciative Inquiry summits (Cooperrider & Whitney, 2005).

Although it is likely that you are most connected with the 'Me' level, these levels of 'Me', 'We' and 'Us' can be integrated for maximal wellbeing effect, and you can also have some impacts on the 'We' and 'Us' levels. For example, in a university setting, a student (Me) can choose to identify and work on their strengths; a team of students (We) can choose to focus on team members' strengths in the deployment of team assignments and projects; and a student could advocate to the university (Us) to choose to invest in the cost of a mindfulness programme for all students. In practice, universities have already started at one or more of these levels and so the challenge is to understand what resources are available at these levels in your local context.

What this systems approach highlights is that assessing wellbeing and intervening at different possible levels within the university community may be a good pathway to increasing your overall and long-term wellbeing and to sustaining it. The language and idea of 'Me', 'We', 'Us' is easily understood and easy to share with your friends, peers, lecturers and other people at university, so it will be useful to keep this framework in the back of your mind for easy reference and explanatory use. You now have the tools to start experimenting at the 'Me' and 'We' levels, to create changes and habits that allow you to begin using your strengths, enhancing your relationships and finding more meaning and engagement at university so you can achieve your potential and maximise your self-care and wellbeing. The next step is for you to take this framework and think about how systems of support and your self-care activities fit into these systems you find yourself in.

Systems of support

All universities have various support systems. Having worked and studied at eight universities between us, we can confidently say that some are much better providers and promoters of these support systems than others. Support entities you can access in the university environment include your lecturers, university administrators, librarians, counsellors, health professionals, clubs and support groups, skills programmes and various helplines. All of these systems have been put in place with the goal of enabling your university experience and success – essentially, to help you excel and succeed. If you do not utilise them when needed, this could impede your success and negatively impact on your wellbeing. So we encourage you to pay specific attention to the details of the support systems at your university – the more you can enact, enable and capitalise on these resources when needed, the better your experience will be. The other important support systems that should not be overlooked are your friends and family. These may be the people who are there for you most when you need help and support, so be proactive and ask for help when you need it.

Putting it into action

Here is a summary of suggested actions from the chapter:

1   See yourself as a scientist and experiment on yourself. You are the expert of you, so experiment on yourself with a range of wellbeing-enhancing activities.
2   Look failure in the face. In line with the topic of positive failure, relish in the learning that can come from experimenting and failing. Remember that trying and failing can lead to development and growth. This positive failure can help to build a platform of enhanced capability where you can reach the place you want to go.
3   Tap into the scientist in you and collect wellbeing data on yourself. Take regular and repeated assessments of your psychological wellbeing over time. Utilise wellbeing assessment data to gauge the impacts of your efforts and help chart a positive growth path forward.
4   Think about how you can change your behaviour for increased wellbeing. What tiny habits can you create to sustain the positive behaviour change you seek?
5   Slow down. Create habits that enable you to slow down. Take three deep breaths often, but in a very controlled way (on the first breath, relax your body; on the second breath, think about what you are grateful for right now; and on the third breath, put your mind into an intentional state).
6   Simplify your life. Aim to do less and prioritise what you do. Think about and cut away some of the non-essential parts of your life – the clutter – to make room for things that are more important and more energising.
7   Think about the systems you find yourself embedded in in the university environment and context. Think about systems beyond yourself and particularly how your self-care activities fit into wider systems of support that can impact on your wellbeing. The 'Me, We, Us' framework can aid your thinking about systems and processes of change.
8   What support systems can you identify? All universities have various support systems: your lecturers, university administrators, librarians, counsellors, health professionals and so on. Pay specific attention to the details of the support systems at your university – the more you can enact, enable and capitalise on these resources when needed, the better your experience will be.

Final thoughts

The skills, knowledge and tools covered in this chapter can supercharge your learning from the rest of this book. Going to university and then beyond are significant life transitions, so we hope that the information provided is useful, and that your experiment turns out well!

Assessment resources

Wellbeing assessment

- Work on Wellbeing: www.workonwellbeing.com
- The PERMA Profiler: https://permahsurvey.com
- Authentic Happiness: www.authentichappiness.sas.upenn.edu/testcenter

Resilience assessment

- Resilience Alliance: www.resalliance.org/resilience-assessment
- Work on Wellbeing: www.workonwellbeing.com

Strengths assessment

- Values in Action (VIA) strengths: www.viacharacter.org
- Strengths Profile: www.strengthsprofile.com

Thirteen

Care about the world

Tim Lomas

Introduction

Going to university can be tough. There are of course many wonderful aspects, from making new connections and lifelong friends to embarking on inspiring intellectual and experiential adventures. But these tend to be interwoven with trickier challenges and, overall, the journey can be quite a rollercoaster. The demands are intense – from pressure to make friends to the need to get good marks – and the stress may feel overwhelming at times. This book contains a wealth of guidance and advice to help you deal with university life. In this chapter, I'd like to offer a suggestion which might sound counter-intuitive and even paradoxical. One of the best ways of caring for yourself and overcoming your issues is caring for other people and helping them address their problems. With that in mind, we will explore research and theory which show the power of caring for others, together with practical recommendations for how to do so.

By the end of the chapter, you will:

- understand that self-care is an important precondition for caring for others
- appreciate that caring for others should ideally be effective and sustainable
- be familiar with various perspectives on the benefit of caring for others
- be able to develop practical plans for how to be more caring in your life.

Self-care comes first

Before we explore the power of caring for the world, there is an important caveat we need to bear in mind from the start: first and foremost, care for yourself. As explored in Chapter 6, try to look after your needs first and foremost, as much as you are able to (recognising of course that some people have caring obligations that are not optional or easily set aside). Crucially, be reassured, this need not be selfish or self-absorbed. Rather, self-care is often a precondition for effectively looking after others. We can think of this as the 'oxygen mask principle'. Think about the instructions you receive on airplanes about putting on your own oxygen mask before helping others to put on theirs. The same principle applies on the ground. If you neglect your own welfare, you put yourself at risk, and potentially others too. Phenomena such as 'compassion fatigue' and 'emotional burnout' are real and need to be guarded against (Sinclair et al., 2017).

So, in thinking about the ideas and recommendations in this chapter, bear this point in mind. If you are beginning to feel depleted in caring for others, take some 'me time' if you can. Make sure you get enough rest. Eat well. Do things that are 'fun', just for your own enjoyment, even if they don't seem 'worthy' (see Chapter 10). Meditate if you find that helpful (see Chapter 7). Make space for your own needs. Again, to reiterate, none of these activities need be thought of as selfish (though of course they could potentially become selfish if one loses sight of the ultimate goal of helping others). Rather, you are recharging your batteries to thereby become more energised for others. You are not being self-absorbed; you are developing your effectiveness.

Aim to be effective

Indeed, the word 'effective' is a helpful touchstone here. It is central to, for instance, an influential new 'effective altruism' movement that has emerged in recent years (check out www.centreforeffectivealtruism.org). It is based on the premise that altruism is good, both for the giver and the recipient. But where the initiative becomes particularly nuanced, interesting and powerful is in its careful, empirically driven considerations on how to make it maximally impactful and sustainable. Consider, for instance, charitable giving. While this is generally laudable, it is also important to do this carefully, so that our money goes as far as possible and does the most good. One issue is where to focus one's resources to be most effective. The 'just one net' campaign recommends that one of the most effective ways of improving people's lives is to help prevent malaria by paying for long-lasting insecticidal nets, which cost just £2 each. Another issue may be how much one should give. From an extreme perspective, the simple answer may be to give everything you own right now, and then volunteer for a charity for free rather than pursuing a lucrative career. But then what? One has nothing more to give, at least for a while. In that sense, better to keep some for yourself so you can live sustainably and continue to contribute in the future. Likewise, rather than forgoing a career to volunteer, it may be more effective to stay in employment and donate a percentage of one's salary. In that respect, the movement's principle is 'giving what we can', with 10% being recognised as the most sustainable amount long term.

So, we ideally want our caring to be sustainable, and moreover not something we do to our detriment. Indeed, it most certainly need not be to our detriment. After all, the central message of this chapter is that caring for the world is not only good for the recipients of our care – though that is of course a laudable and sufficient goal in itself – but benefits us too. As such, bearing in mind the point about making sure you are doing OK, let's explore the ways in which caring is mutually beneficial.

The benefits of caring

We'll start by making the case that caring is indeed beneficial to self and others (before then considering why that may be so). Support for this claim can be found across fields of practice and enquiry, from religious and philosophical traditions to contemporary science.

Beginning with a historical perspective, the importance of caring has been emphasised for millennia by many traditions. In Theravada Buddhism, for instance, four qualities are upheld as being central to psychospiritual development, known collectively as *brahma-viharas* ('divine abidings'). The first three constitute forms of care, namely compassion (*karuṇā*), loving kindness (*mettā*) and sympathetic joy (*muditā*), with the fourth being equanimity (*uppeksha*) (Phelan, 2012). Moreover, of these, compassion is often presented as being pre-eminent, with His Holiness the Dalai Lama calling it the 'essence' of Buddhism, and similarly suggesting that his 'religion is kindness'. In that respect, he writes that 'when we reach beyond the confines of narrow self-interest, our hearts become filled with strength. Peace and joy become our constant companion' (2002, p. 75). Compassion is likewise exalted in Christianity. For instance, St Paul wrote that the three great theological virtues were faith, hope and love (with the latter sometimes rendered alternatively as charity, both being translations of the Greek agape). Again, caring is often presented as being preeminent; as he memorably put it, 'So faith, hope, love abide, these three; but the greatest of these is love' (*Holy Bible*, Revised Standard Version, 1952; 1 Corinthians 13:13).

Similarly, caring has long been valorised by philosophers. Schopenhauer ([1840] 1995), for instance, saw compassion as the foundation for all morality, and the solution to the 'great mystery of ethics' (p. 144). In that respect, he disagreed with thinkers like Kant ([1785] 2002), who suggested that morality was upheld through people rationally assenting to laws, as reflected in the notion of the categorical imperative (i.e. act in ways that you would wish to become a general law). By contrast, Schopenhauer felt that the only viable foundation for a moral framework was the sheer fact that people care in some basic way about the wellbeing of others at all. In the modern age, and building on insights, scholars such as Ozawa-de Silva et al. (2012) identify compassion as 'the most stable foundation for a secular ethics', since it is based on the 'fundamental human aspiration' towards happiness, and thus 'transcends religious, cultural, and philosophical divides' (p. 158). Moreover, the authors have developed a form of 'cognitively based compassion training' to engender such prosocial qualities. Indeed, recent years have seen the emergence of numerous such programmes, such as the 'compassion cultivation training' intervention – created by Stanford's Center for Compassion and Altruism Research and Education – which a randomised controlled trial found to be effective in promoting the three main 'domains' of compassion (compassion for others, self-compassion and receiving compassion) (Jazaieri et al., 2014).

Such developments intersect with contemporary scientific enquiry into the value of caring, both for the carer and the recipient. Unsurprisingly, recipients of care have been shown to benefit in numerous ways, as demonstrated in empirical studies across a range of applied disciplines, from medicine (Sinclair et al., 2020) to leadership (Shuck et al., 2019). Perhaps more significantly, from our perspective here, caring can also benefit the giver (bearing in mind of course the caveats above about the dangers of phenomena like compassion fatigue). For instance, Fredrickson et al. (2008) operationalised a classic Buddhist meditation known as the *metta bhavana* to create a seven-week 'loving kindness' meditation, which they tested in an occupational setting. Corroborating Fredrickson's (2004) 'broaden and build' theory, participants experienced an increase in positive emotions, which in turn built up their personal resources (e.g. purpose in life, social support and mindfulness), subsequently enhancing life satisfaction. Such findings of course raise the fascinating question of why caring should be beneficial in this way, as we explore next.

The dynamics of caring

The idea that caring not only benefits the recipient, but the giver too, might sound surprising or even paradoxical to some. Consider, for instance, compassion, which has an enigmatic, mysterious quality. On the one hand, its etymology defines it as a negative emotional state, deriving from the Latin terms com (with) and pati (to suffer). As Schulz et al. (2007, p. 6) put it, compassion involves 'a sense of shared suffering, combined with a desire to alleviate or reduce such suffering'. This would seem to identify compassion as an unhappy experience that energises the person into striving to reduce or eliminate this state. Yet, it is not uncommon to find qualities like compassion valorised in the most elevated terms, as we saw above. There are various ways to appreciate this counter-intuitive notion, but most centre on an idea which I articulated in a previous article (Lomas, 2015): fundamentally, caring is a radical act of self-transcendence, shifting one's identity from an individualised perspective to a more 'intersubjective' mode of being – from 'me' to 'we'.

Although self-transcendence is a complex and contested construct, it generally means going beyond a narrow idea and experience of the self and entering a more expansive form of identity or experience that encompasses other people. By that, I do not mean the kind of destabilising dissolution of self–other boundaries that may occur in psychopathology (Parnas, 2000). Rather, following the thought of philosopher Georg Hegel ([1807] 1973), it is usually understood as paradoxically involving both the preservation and negation of one's narrow sense of self. In healthy self-transcendence, one can still recognise oneself as a distinct being (self-identity is preserved), but it also expands one's sphere of care and identity to encompass other people (i.e. self-identity is also negated). A powerful instinctual example of transcendence may be a mother with her new baby. Previously, the woman may have had an individualistic sense of selfhood. However, now she may cognitively, emotionally and motivationally experience the baby as an extension of herself (its pain is her pain; its smile is her joy). Yet the mother can still recognise herself as a separate being (in contrast to the baby, who has yet to develop a self–other distinction, and who does experience this dyadic relationship in an 'undifferentiated' way; Mahler et al., 2000). Thus, the mother's individual sense of selfhood has both been preserved (she can still recognise herself as a separate being) and negated (her identity has enlarged to also encompass her child).

In recent decades, numerous concepts and theories have been developed to reflect these kinds of dynamics. In their various ways, these theories suggest that people can transcend a narrow view of selfhood – an autonomous, bounded, individual 'I' – and enter into some kind of experiential union with other people. Perhaps the most well-known is Martin Buber's ([1923] 2004) distinction between 'I-it' and 'I-thou' relationships. With 'I-it' connections – which tend to constitute the majority of people's relationships – the other is regarded instrumentally as an object, valued only to the extent that they fulfil one's own needs. Conversely, in I-thou relationships – in which the other is held in unconditional regard, equally as worthy of love, care and respect as oneself – one enters into a fundamental bond of care. As Buber (1965, p. 170) put it, 'In an essential relation the barriers of individual being are breached and the other becomes present, not merely in the imagination or feeling, but in the depths of one's substance, so that one experiences the mystery of the other being in the mystery of one's own'.

Similar ideas are expressed by other overlapping concepts and theories, including Thich Nhat Hanh's (2000) Buddhist-inspired notion of 'interbeing', the construct of 'identity fusion' (Swann Jr et al., 2009) and models of the self that are intersubjective (De Quincey, 2000), transpersonal (Vaughan, 1985), dialogical (Hermans, 2001) and permeable (Larsen, 1990). For example, De Quincey (2005) proposes three levels of 'intersubjectivity'. The most basic, intersubjectivity-1, occurs through communication, involving the sharing of linguistic signals. This level does not presume any shared identity, but simply involves recognition of the other by virtue of the communicative act. Intersubjectivity-2 then begins to broach the notion of identity shifts; this is the 'communal feeling' one might experience in a meaningful relationship, and particularly during significant moments of interaction (e.g. making love). Finally, intersubjectivity-3 involves a more transformative sense of 'shared presence': this includes a radical identity shift towards a 'more profound transpersonal form of interacting', in which one's 'interrelatedness with another is experienced as primary to one's ontological constitution' (De Quincey, 2005, pp. 34–35).

Crucially, such self-transcendence is regarded by many religious and philosophical traditions – and now contemporary science too – as a powerful pathway towards wellbeing. The context here is that such traditions regard individualised modes of selfhood as a key cause of unhappiness. For example, Buddhism proposes that existence is characterised by three qualities: *anatta* (no-self or insubstantiality), *anicca* (impermanence) and *dukkha* (dissatisfaction or suffering). All phenomena, including humans, are ultimately seen as insubstantial (they are not self-existing entities; their existence depends on a network of supporting conditions) and impermanent (they change as their supporting conditions change). However, people tend to deny *anatta* and *anicca*, and instead regard phenomena, including their own self, as stable and permanent. Crucially, this misperception is seen as a key cause of *dukkha*. This is partly because people become attached to phenomena that are inherently subject to change; people suffer when this change does then occur. It is also because attaching to the idea that one exists as a separate individual generates a constellation of destructive behaviours, from the drive to aggrandise the self (e.g. egotism, pride and jealousy) to the urge to defend and protect it (e.g. hatred and aggression towards anything which threatens it). Similar insights are found in other religious traditions. In that context, such traditions teach that the way to overcome suffering is through self-transcendence (Ho, 1995) – an insight which is also beginning to be corroborated by modern scientific enquiry (Hwang et al., 2019). And, crucially, as argued above, caring for others is a powerful route to such self-transcendence.

Putting it into action

So, the overarching message of this chapter is that caring is good for everyone, including – most significantly here – you yourself as the carer. In that spirit, we will conclude here with some suggestions of how to put this potential into practice. The beautiful part is that there are so many ways to care, and you can pick whichever approach suits you best. You can give time, money or skills – to whatever extent you can share these – to a good cause. At an even more elemental level, you can simply try to be kind to people you encounter, from lending a helping hand if needed to offering a friendly smile as you interact. Nevertheless, even with the possibilities overall being virtually limitless, and each person's situation being unique, we can finish this chapter by offering some general suggestions which might apply to everyone.

First, if you are already motivated to reach out and be caring, then that's great! But if not, and you would like to change that, then don't worry, as there are ways you can. Although people may differ temperamentally in how caring they are, it is not a fixed or static trait, and people can cultivate caring qualities. For instance, above we encountered various practices and interventions that have been developed to help people in these ways.

─────────────────────────── ACTIVITY ───────────────────────────

Practising a loving-kindness meditation 2

Loving-kindness meditation (LKM) was operationalised and assessed by Fredrickson et al. (2008). In a process of guided emotional imagery usually involving five stages, practitioners are encouraged to generate positive feelings for themselves, then extend these outwards, first to a close friend, then to increasingly wide circles of people. You can find instructions for this meditation in Chapter 7. If possible, do try to find a class where you can try it out with the guidance of an experienced teacher. Although it has been generally found to be an effective practice for most people, it can also be quite powerful, and for that very reason, some people can find it challenging (Lomas et al., 2015). As such, it should ideally be learned in a safe and supportive context, with the help of a teacher who can guide you through the process and address any concerns or questions you may have.

Then, once you are imbued with this spirit of caring, you might generally aim to go about expressing this, such as being kind to the people you meet. But it can also be helpful to identify specific strategies to put it into action. Moreover, it will really help if you can find activities that work well for you.

---------------- ACTIVITY ----------------

Discovering and using your strengths

Character strengths are not merely talents or skills you happen to have, but crucially are those which also align with your values and character. For instance, the Values in Action (VIA) framework is a taxonomy of 24 strengths that have been identified as relatively universal (Dahlsgaard et al., 2005). (See Chapter 3 for more detail on VIA.) Once you have completed the VIA test, you can then devise ways to care that align with your strengths. For instance, you might be relatively outgoing and find that your strengths lie in interacting with people. In that case, steer your activities in that direction, such as volunteering to spend time as a mentor, or engaging with older people who are lonely. Or, conversely, you may be relatively quiet and inward but have a passion for creativity and design. You could then offer yourself in ways that reflect these sensibilities. For instance, identify a charity whose mission you believe in and offer your creative input, such as designing a logo or website pro bono. By tailoring your caring in such a way that it reflects who you are and what you value, it is more likely to be meaningful and fulfilling, and moreover, because of that, sustainable and effective.

Final thoughts

As you embrace your university adventure, and beyond, a powerful source of wellbeing lies in caring for other people, and the world more broadly. It may seem counter-intuitive at first, but doing so not only benefits the recipient of our care, but ourselves too. The reasons for these dynamics are complicated, but essentially revolve around the powerful notion of self-transcendence. Caring for others allows us to transcend the usual narrow sense of self-identity that many of us habitually inhabit, and to experience a more expansive selfhood that encompasses others. Crucially, doing so can be a transformative act, not least because those narrow forms of self-identify are seen in many religious and philosophical traditions as a key source of suffering. By taking us 'out of' ourselves and into the world, caring can therefore alleviate these tendencies towards self-preoccupation. That said, we began with the caveat that caring for others depends on self-care, and ideally should not come at the expense of one's own welfare. So, do watch out and take care of yourself first, and guard against the potential for compassion fatigue. But with that consideration in mind, I hope you find ways to cultivate and express the compassion and care that you no doubt already possess within, and in doing so can help improve the world, both for yourself and for those around you.

Fourteen

Conclusion: Savour your experience

Christian van Nieuwerburgh and Paige Williams

Your learning and success

Now that you have reached the end of this book, we're hoping that you feel more positive and better equipped to make the most of your time at university. Based on our experience and the reports of millions of people around the world, the university years are often remembered as a very special time. You may have heard people say that their experience at university was 'the best time of their lives'. University is a place of learning that provides opportunities for students to experiment, to question, to explore and to excel. Lifelong friendships can be created – many people find their life partners at university!

Fundamental to your success at university – whether we're talking about academic achievements, sporting triumphs, social connections or leadership roles – is your personal wellbeing. This book has provided expert insights and practical strategies to ensure both psychological and physical health during your university years. We hope that you have had the opportunity to soak in the learning and to put some of it into practice as a student. All of us (editors and authors) are passionate about your success. More than that, we'd love to think that this book will help you to *enjoy* your time at university.

Reviewing what you can do to thrive

Learning about how you learn

We started by highlighting the value of learning how people learn (Chapter 2). The next few years are going to be characterised by an abundance of learning opportunities – you will be learning about your subject, the extent and limits of individual freedoms, how to relate to others and the best ways of looking after yourself.

Identifying your strengths

Then we discussed the importance of acknowledging and leveraging your character strengths (Chapter 3). Your strengths are strongly connected to your values and principles. University life will provide many contexts in which to use your strengths, understand your values and appreciate the strengths of others.

Being hopeful

We went on to explore the concept of hope, sharing practical ways to increase your hopefulness (Chapter 4). By keeping your focus on a desired future, hope can keep you motivated and will help you to see through some of the more challenging times at university. Hope will support you to set ambitious aspirations and pursue them through the ups and downs of life.

Focusing on what is possible

We also suggested that it will be important for you to focus on what is in your control (Chapter 5). Setting clear goals and understanding how to manage your behaviour effectively will support you to achieve significant outcomes that will build your confidence and sense of self-efficacy.

Looking after yourself

We underscored the critical importance of looking after your wellbeing during this time (Chapter 6). We argue that it is possible for you to be successful at university while also experiencing high levels of subjective wellbeing. It does not have to be an either/or situation. Not only is this possible, it should be the aim.

Living in the moment

One strategy for being more intentional about our wellbeing is mindfulness (Chapter 7). It is possible for you to learn strategies to slow down and be fully present. Not only is this good for your wellbeing, it can help you to study better, connect more deeply with others and enjoy your time at university.

Investing in relationships

A central part of the university experience is other people. We noted the importance of investing in personal relationships as a student (Chapter 8). Building positive relationships is good for your wellbeing and will allow you to start creating social connections and networks that you may benefit from for the rest of your life.

Preparing for adversity

As we alluded to earlier, university life will have moments of joy, frustration, awe and disappointment. Life is unpredictable. We proposed that it is a good idea to prepare for adversity (Chapter 9), putting forward some practical strategies to build your resilience so that you will be better prepared for challenging times at university and throughout your life.

Being playful

A big part of university life for many people is the fun side of things! The good news is that playing and being playful can boost your wellbeing and help you to create meaningful relationships (Chapter 10). As human beings, we are designed to play, so we should do it more often.

Finding meaning

At the same time, human beings are drawn to the concepts of meaning and purpose (Chapter 11). Not only do we want to make sense of the world, we also like to feel that we have a purpose. Your university years are the ideal time to think about these things. Aligning what you are doing and will be doing to something meaningful will be good for your motivation and your wellbeing. Thinking about meaning and purpose will challenge you to reflect on the contribution that you would like to make to the world we live in.

Learning about yourself

In addition to everything you will learn about your chosen subject, this book has highlighted some positive psychology concepts that will support you to thrive at university and beyond. A third subject to learn about is you! We invite you to spend time getting to know yourself better during your time at university (Chapter 12). Understanding yourself better has numerous wellbeing benefits, and positions you better to make meaningful connections with others.

Caring about the world

We share a planet with billions of other people. So far, we haven't been good at caring for the planet. And there is so much more we can do to ensure social justice and fairness in the world we live in. We highlighted the importance of looking beyond our own wellbeing to consider the wellbeing of others (Chapter 13). It is not only the right thing to do, it is necessary for our long-term survival.

Thriving now and in the future

As you consider how you will thrive and support others to do the same, please prioritise your wellbeing. You will experience highs and lows at university. Remember to share positive moments and support others during the highs; look after yourself and seek out support during the lows. While this book provides strategies that will build your resources and resilience to deal with challenges, there may be times when you need external support. It is true that your successes at university will take you far and set you up for a flourishing life. At the same time, any mental health issues that you do not attend to may hold you back in the future. If you feel that you need help, do not hesitate to reach out to personal networks, family members or the support systems provided by your university.

Even though we asked chapter authors to share their areas of expertise, it is notable that some consistent themes emerged. As you focus on your own wellbeing and successes, the question of how you might be of *service* to others is interesting to consider. Chapter authors often referred to the notion of *give and take*, recognising that your experiences at university and beyond will be influenced by your relationships with others. And almost all the chapters invited you to raise your self-awareness. University is an ideal opportunity to get to know yourself better; as you do that, remember to do so with kindness, compassion and love.

We hope that you will thrive at university by being intentional about your wellbeing. This will set you up to have a more positive impact in your personal and professional future. If each of us is able to look after our wellbeing, we will be better placed to support the wellbeing of others. Enjoy what comes next!

Bibliography

Alarcon, G. M., Bowling, N., & Khazon, S. (2013). Great expectations: A meta-analytic examination of optimism and hope. *Personality and Individual Differences*, *54*(7), 821–827.

Alexander, S., & Ussher, S. (2012). The voluntary simplicity movement: A multi-national survey analysis in theoretical context. *Journal of Consumer Culture*, *12*(1), 66–86. https://doi.org/10.1177/1469540512444019

Allen, K.-A., Kern, M. L., Vella-Brodrick, D., Hattie, J., & Waters, L. (2018). What schools need to know about fostering school belonging: A meta-analysis. *Educational Psychology Review*, *30*, 1–34.

Ariga, A., & Lleras, A. (2011). Brief and rare mental 'breaks' keep you focused: Deactivation and reactivation of task goals preempt vigilance decrements. *Cognition*, *118*(3), 439–443. DOI: 10.1016/j.cognition.2010.12.007

Arnott, A. (2013). *Positive failure: Understand how embracing failure is a tool for development*. Cambridge: Cambridge Academic.

Aron, A., Lewandowski, G. W., Jr., Mashek, D., & Aron, E. N. (2013). The self-expansion model of motivation and cognition in close relationships. In J. A. Simpson & L. Campbell (Eds.), *Oxford library of psychology: The Oxford handbook of close relationships* (pp. 90–115). Oxford: Oxford University Press.

Aspinwall, L. G., & Taylor, S. E. (1997). A stitch in time: Self-regulation and proactive coping. *Psychological Bulletin*, *121*, 417–436.

Baer, R. A. (2003). Mindfulness training as a clinical intervention: A conceptual and empirical review. *Clinical Psychology: Science and Practice*, *10*, 125–143.

Bandura, A. (1997). *Self-efficacy: The exercise of control*. New York: W. H. Freeman.

Barrett, L. F. (2017). *How emotions are made: The secret life of the brain*, Chapter 4. New York: Houghton Mifflin Harcourt.

Barrett, L. F. (2020). *Seven and a half lessons about the brain*, Chapter 3. London: Picador.

Basu, A., Duvall, J., & Kaplan, R. (2019). Attention restoration theory: Exploring the role of soft fascination and mental bandwidth. *Environment and Behavior*, *51*(9–10), 1055–1081. https://doi.org/10.1177/0013916518774400

Baumeister, R. F., & Leary, M. R. (1995). The need to belong: Desire for interpersonal attachments as a fundamental human motivation. *Psychological Bulletin*, *11*(3), 497–529.

Becker, C. S. (1992). *Living and relating: An introduction to phenomenology*. London: Sage.

Bennis, W., & Nanus, B. (1985). *Leaders: Strategies for taking charge*. New York: Harper & Row.

Biswas-Diener, R., Kashdan, T. B., & Lyubchik, N. (2017). Psychological strengths at work. In L. G. Oades, M. F. Steger, A. Delle Fave, & J. Passmore (Eds.), *The Wiley Blackwell handbook of the psychology of positivity and strengths-based approaches at work* (pp. 34–47). London: Wiley Online Library.

Biswas-Diener, R., Kashdan, T. B., & Minhas, G. (2011). A dynamic approach to psychological strength development and intervention. *Journal of Positive Psychology, 6*(2), 106–118.

Blackwell, L. S., Trzesniewski, K. H., & Dweck, C. S. (2007). Implicit theories of intelligence predict achievement across an adolescent transition: A longitudinal study and an intervention. *Child Development, 78*(1), 246–263.

Boniwell, I., & Tunariu, A. D. (2019). *Positive psychology: Theory, research and applications* (2nd edn). London: Open University Press/McGraw-Hill Education.

Boyatzis, R. E., & Howard, A. (2013). When goal setting helps and hinders sustained, desired change. In S. David, D. Clutterbuck & D. Megginson (Eds.), *Beyond goals: Effective strategies for coaching and mentoring* (pp. 211–228). London: Routledge.

Brassai, L., Piko, B. F., & Steger, M. F. (2015). A reason to stay healthy: The role of meaning in life in relation to physical activity and healthy eating among adolescents. *Journal of Health Psychology, 20*, 473–482.

Bressi, A. K., & Vaden, E. R. (2017). Reconsidering self-care. *Clinical Social Work Journal, 45*, 33–38.

Brown, K. W., Ryan, R. M., & Creswell, J. D. (2007). Mindfulness: Theoretical foundations and evidence for salutary effects. *Psychological Inquiry, 18*, 211–237.

Brown, S. (2009). *Play: How it shapes the brain, opens the imagination, and invigorates the soul*. New York: Avery.

Brown, S. (2014). Consequences of play deprivation. *Scholarpedia, 9*, 30449.

Bryan, C., O'Sheab, D., & MacIntyrec, T. (2017). Stressing the relevance of resilience: A systematic review of resilience across the domains of sport and work. *International Review of Sport and Exercise Psychology, 12*, 70–111. http://dx.doi.org/10.1080/1750984X.2017.1381140

Buber, M. ([1923] 2004). *I and thou*. New York: Scribner.

Buber, M. (1965). *The knowledge of man: A philosophy of the interhuman*. New York: Harper & Row.

Burke, D., & Linley, P.A. (2007). Enhancing goal self-concordance through coaching. *International Coaching Psychology Review, 2*(1), 62–69.

Calhoun, L. G., & Tedeschi, R. G. (2013). *Posttraumatic growth in clinical practice*. London: Routledge.

Cannon, W. B. (1932). *Wisdom of the body*. New York: W. W. Norton.

Caprara, G. V., Steca, P., Gerbino, M., Paciello, M., & Vecchio, G. M. (2006). Looking for adolescents' well-being: Self-efficacy beliefs as determinants of positive thinking and happiness. *Epidemiology and Psychiatric Sciences, 15*(1), 30–43.

Carlson, L. E., & Speca, M. (2010). *Mindfulness-based cancer recovery*. Oakland, CA: Harbinger.

Carrillo, A., Rubio-Aparicio, M., Molinari, G., Enrique, A., Sanchez-Meca, J., & Banos, R. M. (2019). Effects of the best possible self-intervention: A systematic review and meta-analysis. *PLoS ONE, 14*(9), e0222386. https://doi.org/10.1371/journal.pone.0222386

Carver, C. S., & Connor-Smith, J. (2010). Personality and coping. *Annual Review of Psychology, 61*, 679–704.

Chadwick, P. (2014). Mindfulness for psychosis. *British Journal of Psychiatry, 204*, 333–334.

Chamberlain, K., & Zika, S. (1988). Religiosity, life meaning, and wellbeing: Some relationships in a sample of women. *Journal for the Scientific Study of Religion, 27*, 411–420.

Chang, E. C. (1998). Hope, problem solving ability, and coping in a college population: Some implications for theory and practice. *Journal of Clinical Psychology, 54*(7), 953–962.

Cheavens, J. S., Feldman, D. B., Gum, A., Michael, S. T., & Snyder, C. R. (2006). Hope therapy in a community sample: A pilot investigation. *Social Indicators Research, 77*, 61–78.

Chiesa, A., & Serretti, A. (2010). A systematic review of neurobiological and clinical features of mindfulness meditations. *Psychological Medicine, 40*, 1239–1252.

Chiesa, A., & Serretti, A. (2011). Mindfulness based cognitive therapy for psychiatric disorders: A systematic review and meta-analysis. *Psychiatry Research, 187*(3), 441–453.

Chiesa, A., Anselmi, R., & Serretti, A. (2014). Psychological mechanisms of mindfulness-based interventions: What do we know? *Holistic Nursing Practice, 28*(2), 124–148.

Chmitorz, A., Kunzler, A., Helmreich, I., Tüscher, O., Kalisch, R., Kubiak, T., Wessa, M., & Lieb, K. (2018). Intervention studies to foster resilience: A systematic review and proposal for a resilience framework in future intervention studies. *Clinical Psychology Review, 59*, 78–100. http://dx.doi.org/10.1016/j.cpr.2017.11.002

Cohen, R., Bavishi, C., & Rozanski, A. (2016). Purpose in life and its relationship to all-cause mortality and cardiovascular events: A meta-analysis. *Psychosomatic Medicine, 78*(2), 122–133.

Compas, B. E., Connor-Smith, J. K., Saltzman, H, Thomsen, A. H., & Wadsworth, M. E. (2001). Coping with stress during childhood and adolescence: Problems, progress, and potential in theory and research. *Psychological Bulletin, 127*, 87–127.

Cooperrider, D., & Whitney, D. (2005). *Appreciative inquiry: A positive revolution in change*. San Francisco, CA: Berrett-Koehler.

Creswell, J. D. (2017). Mindfulness interventions. *Annual Review of Psychology, 68*, 491–516.

Csikszentmihalyi, M. (2008). *Flow: The psychology of optimal experience*. New York: Harper Perennial.

Dahlsgaard, K., Peterson, C., & Seligman, M. E. P. (2005). Shared virtue: The convergence of valued human strengths across culture and history. *Review of General Psychology, 9*(3), 203–213.

Daniels, K., & Guppy, A. (1997). Stressors, locus of control, and social support as consequences of affective psychological well-being. *Journal of Occupational Health Psychology, 2*(2), 156–174.

Davachi, L., Kiefer, T., Rock, D., & Rock, L. (2010). Learning that lasts through AGES. *NeuroLeadership Journal, 3*, 1–11. Available at: www.academia.edu/36742185/Learning_that_lasts_through_AGES

David, S. (2018). *Emotional agility: Get unstuck, embrace change and thrive in work and life*. New York: Penguin.

Davidson, O. B., Feldman, D. B., & Margalit, M. (2012). A focused intervention for 1st year college students: Promoting hope, sense of coherence, and self-efficacy. *Journal of Psychology, 146*(3), 333–353.

De Quincey, C. (2000). Intersubjectivity: Exploring consciousness from the second-person perspective. *Journal of Transpersonal Psychology, 32*(2), 135–156.

De Quincey, C. (2005). *Radical knowing: Understanding consciousness through relationship*. South Paris, ME: Park Street Press.

Didonna, F. (2009). *Clinical handbook of mindfulness*. New York: Springer.

Diekelmann, S., Wilhelm, I., & Born, J. (2009). The whats and whens of sleep-dependent memory. *Sleep Medicine Reviews, 13*, 309–321.

Dieleman, H., & Huisingh, D. (2006). Games by which to learn and teach about sustainable development: Exploring the relevance of games and experiential learning for sustainability. *Journal of Cleaner Production, 14*, 837–847.

Dixson, D. D., Keltner, D., Worrell, F. C., & Mello, Z. (2018). The magic of hope: Hope mediates the relationship between socioeconomic status and academic achievement. *Journal of Educational Research, 111*(4), 507–515. http://dx.doi.org/10.1080/00220671.2017.1302915

Dubinsky, J. M., Guzey, S. S., Schwartz, M. S., Roehrig, G., MacNabb, C., Schmied, A., ... & Ellingson, C. (2019). Contributions of neuroscience knowledge to teachers and their practice. *The Neuroscientist, 25*(5), 394–407.

Duncan, L. G., & Bardacke, N. (2010). Mindfulness-based childbirth and parenting education: Promoting family mindfulness during the perinatal period. *Journal of Child and Family Studies, 19*(2), 190–202.

Dutton, J., & Heaphy, E. (2003). The power of high quality connections. In K. Cameron, J. Dutton & R. Quinn (Eds.), *Positive organizational scholarship: Foundations of a new discipline* (pp. 263–278). San Francisco, CA: Berrett-Koehler.

Duval, S., & Wicklund, R. A. (1972). *A theory of objective self-awareness*. New York: Academic Press.

Duvall, J., & Sullivan, W. (2016). How to get more out of the green exercise experience: Insights from attention restoration theory. In J. Barton, R. Bragg, C. Wood & J. Pretty (Eds.), *Green exercise linking nature, health and well-being* (pp. 37–45). London: Routledge.

Dweck, C. (2017). *Mindset: Changing the way you think to fulfil your potential*. London: Hachette UK.

Dyer, S., & Moneta, G. B. (2006). Frequency of parallel, associative, and cooperative play in British children of different socio-economic status. *Social Behavior and Personality*, *34*(5), 587–592.

Edwards, M., & van Tongeren, D. R. (2020). Meaning mediates the association between suffering and well-being. *Journal of Positive Psychology*, *15*, 722–733.

Emmons, R. A. (1992). Abstract versus concrete goals: Personal striving level, physical illness, and psychological well-being. *Journal of Personality and Social Psychology*, *62*(2), 292–300.

Feeney, B. C. (2007). The dependency paradox in close relationships: Accepting dependence promotes independence. *Journal of Personality and Social Psychology*, *92*(2), 268–285.

Feeney, J. A. (2008). Adult romantic attachment: Developments in the study of couple relationships. In J. Cassidy & P. R. Shaver (Eds.), *Handbook of attachment: Theory, research, and clinical applications* (pp. 456–481). New York: Guilford Press.

Feldman, D. B., & Dreher, D. E. (2012). Can hope be changed in 90 minutes? Testing the efficacy of a single-session goal-pursuit intervention for college students. *Journal of Happiness Studies*, *13*, 745–759.

Feldman, D. B., & Snyder, C. R. (2005). Hope and the meaningful life: Theoretical and empirical associations between goal-directed thinking and life meaning. *Journal of Social and Clinical Psychology*, *24*, 401–421.

Feldman, D. B., Rand, K. L., & Kahle-Wrobleski, K. (2009). Hope and goal attainment: Testing a basic prediction of hope theory. *Journal of Social and Clinical Psychology*, *28*(4), 479–497.

Ferrara, M., Iaria, G., De Gennaro, L., Guariglia, C., Curcio, G., Tempesta, D., & Bertini, M. (2006). The role of sleep in the consolidation of rote learning in humans: A behavioural study. *Brain Research Bulletin*, *71*, 4–9.

Fiske, S. T. (2018). *Social beings: A core motives approach to social psychology* (4th edn). Hoboken, NJ: Wiley.

Fletcher, D., & Sarkar, M. (2016). Mental fortitude training: An evidence-based approach to developing psychological resilience for sustained success. *Journal of Sport Psychology in Action*, *7*(3), 135–157. https://doi.org/10.1080/21520704. 2016.1255496

Fogg, B. J. (2020). *Tiny habits: The small changes that change everything*. New York: Houghton Mifflin Harcourt.

Folkman, S., & Moskowitz, J. T. (2004). Coping: Pitfalls and promise. *Annual Review of Psychology*, *55*, 745–774.

Frankl, V. E. (1963). *Man's search for meaning: An introduction to logotherapy*. New York: Washington Square Press.

Frazier, P., Tennen, H., & Meredith, L. (2017). Three generations of research on perceived control. In J. W. Reich & F. J. Infurna (Eds.), *Perceived control: Theory, research, and practice in the first 50 years* (pp. 171–199). New York: Oxford University Press.

Fredrickson, B. L. (2004). The broaden-and-build theory of positive emotions. *Philosophical Transactions of the Royal Society of London. Series B: Biological Sciences*, *359*(1449), 1367–1377.

Fredrickson, B. L., Cohn, M. A., Coffey, K. A., Pek, J., & Finkel, S. M. (2008). Open hearts build lives: Positive emotions, induced through loving-kindness meditation, build consequential personal resources. *Journal of Personality and Social Psychology, 95*(5), 1045–1062. https://doi.org/10.1037/a0013262

Friedman, H. S., & Kern, M. L. (2012). Psychological predictors of heart disease. In V. S. Ramachandran (Editor-in-Chief), *Encyclopedia of human behavior* (2nd edn). San Diego, CA: Elsevier.

Friese, M., Messner, C., & Schaffner, Y. (2012). Mindfulness meditation counteracts self-control depletion. *Consciousness and Cognition, 21*, 1016–1022.

Frydenberg, E. (2017). *Coping and the challenge of resilience*. London: Palgrave Macmillan.

Gál, É., Ştefan, S., & Cristea, I. A. (2021). The efficacy of mindfulness meditation apps in enhancing users' well-being and mental health related outcomes: A meta-analysis of randomized controlled trials. *Journal of Affective Disorders, 279*, 131–142.

Gallagher, M. W., & Lopez, S. J. (2009). Positive expectancies and mental health: Identifying the unique contributions of hope and optimism. *Journal of Positive Psychology, 4*(6), 548–556.

Gallagher, M. W., & Lopez, S. J. (2018). Introduction to the science of hope. In M. W. Gallagher & S. J. Lopez (Eds.), *The Oxford Handbook of Hope*. Oxford: Oxford University Press.

Gallagher, M. W., Marques, S. C., & Lopez, S. J. (2017). Hope and the academic trajectory of college students. *Journal of Happiness Studies, 18*, 341–352.

Gander, F., Hofmann, J., Proyer, R. T., & Ruch, W. (2019). Character strengths: Stability, change, and relationships with well-being changes. *Applied Research in Quality of Life, 15*, 349–367.

Gaskins, S., Haight, W., & Lancy, D. F. (2007). The cultural construction of play. In A. Göncü & S. Gaskins (Eds.), *Play and development: Evolutionary, sociocultural, and functional perspectives* (pp. 179–202). Mahwah, NJ: Lawrence Erlbaum.

Gelso, C. J., Williams, E. N., & Fretz, B. (2014). *Counseling psychology* (3rd edn). Washington, DC: American Psychological Association.

Goodman, F. R., Disabato, D. J., Kashdan, T. B., & Machell, K. A. (2017). Personality strengths as resilience: A one-year multiwave study. *Journal of Personality, 85*(3), 423–434.

Goodman, J. H., Guarino, A., Chenausky, K., Klein, L., Prager, J., Petersen, R., Forget, A., & Freeman, M. (2014). CALM Pregnancy: Results of a pilot study of mindfulness-based cognitive therapy for perinatal anxiety. *Archives of Women's Mental Health, 17*(5), 373–387.

Grah, B., & Dimovski, V. (2014). Neuroleadership and an advanced learning organization. E-Leader. www.g-casa.com/conferences/milan/paper/Grah.pdf

Graham, J. E., Christian, L. M., & Kiecolt-Glaser, J. K. (2006). Stress, age, and immune function: Toward a lifespan approach. *Journal of Behavioral Medicine, 29*, 389–400.

Grant, A. (2016). *Originals: How non-conformists change the world*. London: Penguin Random House.

Green, S. (2019). *The positive prescription: A 6-week wellbeing program based on the science of positive psychology*. Double Bay, NSW: Suzy Green/The Positivity Institute.

Grossman, P., Niemann, L., Schmidt, S., & Walach, H. (2004). Mindfulness-based stress reduction and health benefits. A meta-analysis. *Journal of psychosomatic research, 57*(1), 35–43. https://doi.org/10.1016/S0022-3999(03)00573-7

Halvorson, H. G., Cox, C., & Rock, D. (2016). Organizational growth mindset. *NeuroLeadership Journal, 6*, 3–13.

Hamann, G. A., & Ivtzan, I. (2016). 30 minutes in nature a day can increase mood, well-being, meaning in life and mindfulness: Effects of a pilot programme. *Social Inquiry into Well-Being, 2*(2), 34–46. https://doi.org/10.13165/SIIW-16-2-2-04

Hart, R., Ivtzan, I., & Hart, D. (2013). Mind the gap in mindfulness research: A comparative account of the leading schools of thought. *Review of General Psychology, 17*(4), 453–466. https://doi.org/10.1037/a0035212

Hausler, M., Strecker, C., Huber, A., Brenner, M., Höge, T., & Höfer, S. (2017). Associations between the application of signature character strengths, health and well-being of health professionals. *Frontiers in Psychology, 8*. https://doi-org.ezproxy.rgu.ac.uk/10.3389/fpsyg.2017.01307

Hayes, S. C., Strosahl, K., & Wilson, K. G. (1999). *Acceptance and commitment therapy: An experiential approach to behaviour change*. New York: Guilford Press.

Health and Productivity Institute of Australia (HAPIA) (2009). *Best practice guidelines: Workplace health in Australia*. Sydney, NSW: HAPIA.

Hebb, D. O. (1949). *The organisation of behaviour: a neuropsychological theory*. New York: Science Editions.

Hedtke, L. (2014). Creating stories of hope: A narrative approach to illness, death and grief. *Australia and New Zealand Journal of Family Therapy, 35*, 4–19.

Hefferon, K. (2012). Bringing back the body into positive psychology: The theory of corporeal posttraumatic growth in breast cancer survivorship. *Psychology, 3*(12), 1238–1242. https://doi.org/10.4236/psych.2012.312A183

Hefferon, K., & Kampman, H. (2020). Taking an embodied approach to post-traumatic growth research and sport. In R. Wadey, D. Melissa & K. Howells (Eds.), *Growth following adversity in sport: A mechanism to positive change* (pp. 131–144). London: Routledge.

Hefferon, K., Grealy, M., & Mutrie, N. (2009). Post-traumatic growth and life threatening physical illness: A systematic review of the qualitative literature. *British Journal of Health Psychology, 14*(2), 343–378. https://doi.org/10.1348/135910708X332936

Hegel, G. W. F. ([1807] 1973). *Phenomenology of mind*. Frankfurt: Verlag Ullstein.

Hermans, H. J. M. (2001). The dialogical self: Toward a theory of personal and cultural positioning. *Culture & Psychology, 7*(3), 243–281. https://doi.org/10.1177/1354067X0173001

His Holiness The Dalai Lama (2002). Understanding our fundamental nature. In J. Davidson & A. Harrington (Eds.), *Visions of compassion: Western scientists and Tibetan Buddhists examine human nature* (pp. 66–80). Oxford: Oxford University Press.

Ho, D. Y. F. (1995). Selfhood and identity in Confucianism, Taoism, Buddhism, and Hinduism: Contrasts with the West. *Journal for the Theory of Social Behaviour, 25*(2), 115–139.

Hobfoll, S. E. (1989). Conservation of resources: A new attempt at conceptualizing stress. *American Psychologist, 44*, 513–524.

Hobfoll, S. E. (1998). *Stress, culture, and community.* New York: Plenum.

Hobfoll, S. E. (2002). Social and psychological resources and adaptation. *Review of General Psychology, 6*(4), 307–324.

Hobfoll, S. E., Hall, B. J., Canetti-Nisim, D., Galea, S., Johnson, R. J., & Palmieri, P. A. (2007). Refining our understanding of traumatic growth in the face of terrorism: Moving from meaning cognitions to doing what is meaningful. *Applied Psychology, 56*(3), 345–366. https://doi.org/10.1111/j.1464-0597.2007.00292.x

Honoré, C. (2004). *In praise of slow: How a worldwide movement is challenging the cult of speed.* Toronto: A. A. Knopf Canada.

Huppert, F. A., & So, T. T. C. (2013). Flourishing across Europe: Application of a new conceptual framework for defining well-being. *Social Indicators Research, 110*, 837–861.

Hwang, H., Tu, C., & Chan, H. (2019). Self-transcendence, caring and their associations with well-being. *Journal of Advanced Nursing, 75*(7), 1473–1483. https://doi.org/10.1111/jan.13937

IJntema, R. C., Burger, Y. D., & Schaufeli, W. B. (2019). Reviewing the labyrinth of psychological resilience: Establishing criteria for resilience-building programs. *Consulting Psychology Journal: Practice and Research, 71*(4), 288–304. https://doi.org/10.1037/cpb0000147

Illeris, K. (2010). Characteristics of adult learning. In P. Peterson, E. Baker & B. McGaw (Eds.), *International encyclopaedia of education* (3rd edn, pp. 36–41). Oxford: Elsevier.

Immordino-Yang, M. H., & Fischer, K. W. (2010). Neuroscience bases for learning. In P. Peterson, E. Baker & B. McGaw (Eds.), *International encyclopaedia of education* (3rd edn, pp. 310–316). Oxford: Elsevier.

Ivtzan, I., & Hart, R. (2015). Mindfulness scholarship and interventions: A review. In A. L. Baltzell (Ed.), *Mindfulness and performance* (pp. 3–29). Cambridge: Cambridge University Press.

Ivtzan, I., & Lomas, T. (Eds.) (2016). *Mindfulness in positive psychology: The science of meditation and wellbeing.* London: Routledge.

Janoff-Bulman, R. (1992). *Shattered assumptions: Towards a new psychology of trauma.* London: Simon & Schuster.

Jarden, A., & Jarden, R. (2016). Positive psychological assessment for the workplace. In L. Oades, M. F. Steger, A. Delle Fave & J. Passmore (Eds.), *The Wiley-Blackwell handbook of positive psychology at work* (pp. 415–437). London: Wiley Online Library.

Jazaieri, H., McGonigal, K., Jinpa, T., Doty, J. R., Gross, J. J., & Goldin, P. R. (2014). A randomized controlled trial of compassion cultivation training: Effects on mindfulness, affect, and emotion regulation. *Motivation and Emotion, 38*(1), 23–35. https://doi.org/10.1007/s11031-013-9368-z

Jim, H. S., Purnell, J. Q., Richardson, S. A., Golden-Kreutz, D. & Andersen, B. L. (2006). Measuring meaning in life following cancer. *Quality of Life Research, 15*, 1355–1371.

Joseph, S. (2012). *What doesn't kill us: The new psychology of posttraumatic growth*. London: Piatkus.

Joyce, S., Shand, F., Tighe, J., Laurent, S. J., Bryant, R. A., & Harvey, S. B. (2018). Road to resilience: A systematic review and meta-analysis of resilience training programmes and interventions. *BMJ Open, 8*(6), e017858. https://doi.org/10.1136/bmjopen-2017-017858

Kabat-Zinn, J. (1982). An outpatient program in behavioral medicine for chronic pain patients based on the practice of mindfulness meditation: Theoretical considerations and preliminary results. *General Hospital Psychiatry, 4*, 33–47.

Kabat-Zinn, J. (1994). *Wherever you go, there you are: Mindfulness meditation in everyday life*. New York: Hyperion.

Kabat-Zinn, J. (2003). Mindfulness-based interventions in context: Past, present, and future. *Clinical Psychology: Science and Practice, 10*, 144–156.

Kabat-Zinn, J. (2005). *Coming to our senses*. London: Piatkus Books.

Kabat-Zinn, J., Massion, A. O., Kristeller, J., Peterson, L. G., Fletcher, K., Fletcher, K.E., Pbert, L., Lenderking, W. R., & Santorelli, S. F. (1992). Effectiveness of a meditation based stress reduction program in the treatment of anxiety disorders. *American Journal of Psychiatry, 149*, 936–943.

Kabat-Zinn, J., Wheeler, E., & Light, T. (1998). Influence of a mindfulness meditation based stress reduction intervention on rates of skin clearing in patients. *Psychosomatic Medicine, 60*, 625–632.

Kampman, H., & Hefferon, K. (2020). 'Find a sport and carry on': Posttraumatic growth and achievement in British Paralympic athletes. *International Journal of Wellbeing, 10*(1), article 1. https://doi.org/10.5502/ijw.v10i1.765

Kampman, H., Hefferon, K., Wilson, M., & Beale, J. (2015). 'I can do things now that people thought were impossible, actually, things that I thought were impossible': A meta-synthesis of the qualitative findings on posttraumatic growth and severe physical injury. *Canadian Psychology/Psychologie Canadienne, 56*(3), 283–294. https://doi.org/10.1037/cap0000031

Kant, I. ([1785] 2002). *Groundwork for the metaphysics of morals*. New Haven, CT: Yale University Press.

Kaplan, R., & Kaplan, S. (1989). *The experience of nature: A psychological perspective*. Cambridge: Cambridge University Press.

Kauffman, C., & Scoular, A. (2004). Toward a positive psychology of executive coaching. In P. Linley & S. Joseph (Eds.), *Positive practice in psychology* (pp. 287–304). Hoboken, NJ: Wiley.

Kayes, D. C. (2006). The problem of goalodicy: The unintended consequences of goal pursuit. In *Destructive goal pursuit: The Mount Everest disaster* (pp. 41–50). Berlin: Springer.

Kemeny, M. E. (2007). Psychoneuroimmunology. In H. S. Friedman & R. C. Silver (Eds.), *Foundations of health psychology* (pp. 92–116). New York: Oxford University Press.

Keng, S. L., Smoski, M. J., & Robins, C. J. (2011). Effects of mindfulness on psychological health: A review of empirical studies. *Clinical Psychology Review, 31*, 1041–1056.

Kern, M. L., Williams, P., Spong, C., Colla, R., Sharma, K., Downie, A., ... & Oades, L. G. (2020). Systems informed positive psychology. *Journal of Positive Psychology, 15*(6), 705–715. https://doi.org/10.1080/17439760.2019.1639799

Keyes, C. L. M. (2011). Authentic purpose: The spiritual infrastructure of life. *Journal of Management, Spirituality & Religion, 8*(4), 281–297.

Kim, E. S., Strecher, V. J., & Ryff, C. D. (2014). Purpose in life and use of preventive health care services. *PNAS, 111*, 331–336.

Kim, S. H. (2014). Evidence-based (simple but effective) advice for college students: Microaction and macrochange. *The Mentor: Innovative Scholarship on Academic Advising, 16*. DOI: 10.26209/MJ1661262

King, L. A. (2001). The health benefits of writing about life goals. *Personality and Social Psychology Bulletin, 27*(7), 798–807.

Kramer, G. P., Bernstein, D. A., & Phares, V. (2013). *Introduction to clinical psychology* (8th edn). New York: Pearson Education.

Krause, N., & Hayward, R. D. (2012). Religion, meaning in life, and change in physical functioning during late adulthood. *Journal of Adult Development, 19*(3), 158–169.

Kristeller, J. L., & Wolever, R. Q. (2010). Mindfulness-based eating awareness training for treating binge eating disorder: The conceptual foundation. *Eating Disorders, 19*(1), 49–61.

Kubey, R. W., & Csikszentmihalyi, M. (1990) Television as escape: Subjective experience before an evening of heavy viewing. *Communication Reports, 3*, 92–100.

Laing, R. D. (1959/1965). *The divided self: An existential study in sanity and madness*. Harmondsworth: Penguin.

Lally, P., van Jaarsveld, C. H. M., Potts, H. W. W., & Wardle, J. (2010). How are habits formed: Modelling habit formation in the real world. *European Journal of Social Psychology, 40*(6), 998–1009. https://doi.org/10.1002/ejsp.674

Lambert, N. M., Stillman, T. F., Hicks, J. A., Kamble, S., Baumeister, R. F., & Fincham, F. D. (2013). To belong is to matter: Sense of belonging enhances meaning in life. *Personality and Social Psychology Bulletin, 39*(11), 1418–1427.

Larsen, S. (1990). Our inner cast of characters. *The Humanistic Psychologist, 18*(2), 176–187.

Latham, G., Seijts, G., & Slocum, J. (2016) The goal setting and goal orientation labyrinth. *Organizational Dynamics, 4*(45), 271–277.

Law, A. S., Logie, R. H., & Pearson, D. G. (2006). The impact of secondary tasks on multitasking in a virtual environment. *Acta Psychologica, 122*, 27–44.

Lazarus, R. S., & Folkman, S. (1984). *Stress, appraisal, and coping*. New York: Springer.

Lee, J. Y., & Gallagher, M. W. (2018). Hope and wellbeing. In M. W. Gallagher & S. J. Lopez (Eds.), *The Oxford handbook of hope* (pp. 287–298). Oxford: Oxford University Press.

Lepore, S. J., & Revenson, T. A. (2006). Resilience and posttraumatic growth: Recovery, resistance, and reconfiguration. In L. G. Calhoun & R. G. Tedeschi (Eds.), *Handbook of posttraumatic growth: Research and practice* (pp. 24–46). Mahwah, NJ: Lawrence Erlbaum.

Lewis, H. R. (2004). Slow down: Getting more out of Harvard by doing less. https://lewis.seas.harvard.edu/files/harrylewis/files/slowdown2004_0.pdf

Linehan, M. (1993). *Cognitive-behavioral therapy of borderline personality disorder*. New York: Guilford Press.

Linley, A. (2008). *Average to A+: Realising strengths in yourself and others*. Coventry: CAPP Press.

Linley, A., & Harrington, S. (2006). Playing to your strengths. *The Psychologist, 19*(2), 86–89.

Linley, P. A., & Joseph, S. (2004). Applied positive psychology: A new perspective for professional practice. In P. A. Linley & S. Joseph (Eds.), *Positive psychology in practice* (pp. 3–12). Hoboken, NJ: John Wiley & Sons.

Little, B. R. (1989) Personal projects analysis: Trivial pursuits, magnificent obsessions, and the search for coherence. In D. M. Buss & N. Cantor (Eds.), *Personality psychology: Recent trends and emerging directions* (pp. 15–31). New York: Springer.

Locke, E. A., & Latham, G. P. (2002). Building a practically useful theory of goal setting and task motivation: A 35-year odyssey. *American Psychologist, 57*(9), 705–717.

Locke, E. A. & Latham, G. P. (2006). New directions in goal-setting theory. *Current Directions in Psychological Science, 15*(5), 265–268.

Lomas, T. (2015). Self-transcendence through shared suffering: An intersubjective theory of compassion. *Journal of Transpersonal Psychology, 47*(2), 168–187.

Lomas, T., Cartwright, T., Edginton, T., & Ridge, D. (2015). A qualitative analysis of experiential challenges associated with meditation practice. *Mindfulness, 6*(4), 848–860. https://doi.org/10.1007/s12671-014-0329-8

Long, K., & Bonanno, G. A. (2018). An integrative temporal framework for psychological resilience. In J. G. Noll & I. Shalev (Eds.), *The biology of early life stress: Understanding child maltreatment and trauma* (pp. 121–146). New York: Springer International. https://doi.org/10.1007/978-3-319-72589-5_8

Lopez, S. J. (2013). *Making hope happen: Create the future you want for yourself and others*. New York: Atria Books.

Lopez, S. J., Ciarelli, R., Coffman, L., Stone, M., & Wyatt, L. (2000). Diagnosing for strengths: On measuring hope building blocks. In C. R. Snyder (Ed.), *Handbook of hope: Theory, measures and application* (pp. 57–85). San Diego, CA: Academic Press.

Lu, L., & Argyle, M. (1994). Leisure satisfaction and happiness: A function of leisure activity. *Kaohsiung Journal of Medical Sciences, 10*(2), 89–96.

Luepnitz, D. A. (2002). *Schopenhauer's porcupines: Intimacy and its dilemmas – Five stories of psychotherapy*. New York: Basic Books.

Magnuson, C. D., & Barnett, L. A. (2013). The playful advantage: How playfulness enhances coping with stress. *Leisure Sciences, 35*, 129–144.

Magyar-Moe, J. L., & Lopez, S. J. (2015). Strategies for accentuating hope. In P. A. Linley & S. Joseph (Eds.), *Positive psychology in practice: Promoting human flourishing in work, health, education, and everyday life* (2nd edn, pp. 483–502). London: Wiley.

Mahler, M. S., Pine, F., & Bergman, A. (2000). *The psychological birth of the human infant symbiosis and individuation*. New York: Basic Books.

Maisel, N. C., & Gable, S. L. (2009). The paradox of received social support: The importance of responsiveness. *Psychological Science, 20*(8), 928–932.

Majors, K., & Baines, E. (2017). Children's play with their imaginary companions: Parent experiences and perceptions of the characteristics of the imaginary companions and purposes served. *Education & Child Psychology, 34*(3), 37–56.

Marchand, W. R. (2012). MBSR, mindfulness-based cognitive therapy, and Zen meditation for depression, anxiety, pain, and psychological distress. *Journal of Psychiatric Practice, 18*, 233–252.

Marques, S. C., Gallagher, M. W., & Lopez, S. J. (2017). Hope and academic-related outcomes: A meta-analysis. *School Mental Health, 9*, 250–262.

Marques, S. C., Lopez, S. J., Fontaine, A. M., Coimbra, S., & Mitchell, J. (2015). How much hope is enough? Levels of hope and students' psychological and school functioning. *Psychology in the Schools, 52*(4), 325–334.

Martela, F., & Steger, M. F. (2016). The three meanings of meaning in life: Distinguishing coherence, purpose and significance. *Journal of Positive Psychology, 11*, 531–545.

Martin-Krumm, C., Delas, Y., Lafrenière, M., Fenouillet, F., & Lopez, S. (2015). The structure of the State Hope Scale. *Journal of Positive Psychology, 10*(3), 272–281.

Martínez-Martí, M. L., & Ruch, W. (2014). Character strengths and well-being across the life span: Data from a representative sample of German-speaking adults living in Switzerland. *Frontiers in Psychology, 5*, 1253. DOI: 10.3389/fpsyg.2014.01253

Martínez-Martí, M. L., & Ruch, W. (2017). Character strengths predict resilience over and above positive affect, self-efficacy, optimism, social support, self-esteem, and life satisfaction. *Journal of Positive Psychology, 12*(2), 110–119. https://doi-10.1080/17439760.2016.1163403

Mascaro, N., & Rosen, D. H. (2005). Existential meaning's role in the enhancement of hope and prevention of depressive symptoms. *Journal of Personality, 73*(4), 985–1013.

Mashek, D. J., & Aron, A. (Eds.) (2004). *Handbook of closeness and intimacy*. Mahwah, NJ: Lawrence Erlbaum.

Maslach, C., Schaufeli, W. B., & Leiter, M. P. (2001). Job burnout. *Annual Review of Psychology, 52*, 397–422.

Mazza, P. (1997). Keeping it simple. *Reactions, 36*, 10–12.

McCann, J. T., & Biaggio, M. K. (1989). Sexual satisfaction in marriage as a function of life meaning. *Archives of Sexual Behavior, 18*, 59–72.

McEwen, B. S. (1993). Stress, adaptation, and disease: Allostasis and allostatic load. *Annals of the New York Academy of Sciences, 840*, 33–44.

McKnight, P.E. & Kashdan, T.B. (2009). Purpose in life as a system that creates and sustains health and well-being: An integrative, testable theory. *Review of General Psychology, 13*(3), 242–251.

McQuaid, M., & Kern, M. L. (2017). *Your wellbeing blueprint: Feeling good and doing well at work.* Melbourne, VIC: McQuaid Ltd.

Merriam, S. B. (2010). Adult learning. In P. Peterson, E. Baker & B. McGaw (Eds.), *International encyclopaedia of education* (3rd edn, pp. 12–17). Oxford: Elsevier.

Mikulincer, M., & Goodman, G. S. (Eds.) (2006). *Dynamics of romantic love: Attachment, caregiving, and sex.* New York: Guildford Press.

Mikulincer, M., & Shaver, P. R. (2007). *Attachment in adulthood: Structure, dynamics, and change.* New York: Guildford Press.

Miller, M., & Byers, J. (1998). Sparring as play in young pronghorn males. In M. Berkoff & J. A. Byers (Eds.), *Animal play: Evolutionary, comparative, and ecological perspectives* (pp. 141–160). Cambridge: Cambridge University Press.

Moos, R. H., & Schaefer, J. A. (1993). Coping resources and processes: Current concepts and measures. In L. Goldberger & S. Breznitz (Eds.), *Handbook of stress: Theoretical and clinical aspects* (2nd edn, pp. 234–257). New York: Free Press.

Neff, K. (2003). Self-compassion: An alternative conceptualization of a healthy attitude toward oneself. *Self and Identity, 2,* 85–101.

Nhat Hanh, T. (2000). *The path of emancipation.* Berkeley, CA: Parallax Press.

Niemiec, R. (2013). *Mindfulness and character strengths: A practical guide to flourishing.* Gottingenv: Hogrefe Publishing.

Niemiec, R. (2018). *Character strengths interventions: A field guide for practitioners.* Boston, MA: Hogrefe Publishing.

Niemiec, R. (2019). Finding the golden mean: The overuse, underuse, and optimal use of character strengths. *Counselling Psychology Quarterly, 32*(3–4), 453–471. https://doi.org/10.1080/09515070.2019.1617674

Norrish, J. M. (2015). *Positive education: The Geelong Grammar School journey.* Oxford Positive Psychology Series. Oxford: Oxford University Press.

Nusbaum, E. C., & Silvia, P. J. (2011). Are intelligence and creativity really so different? Fluid intelligence, executive processes and strategy use in divergent thinking. *Intelligence, 39,* 36–45.

Olendzki, A. (2009). Mindfulness and meditation. In F. Didonna (Ed.), *Clinical handbook of mindfulness* (pp. 37–44). New York: Springer.

Ong, J., & Sholtes, D. (2010). A mindfulness-based approach to the treatment of insomnia. *Journal of Clinical Psychology, 66*(11), 1175–1184.

Ozawa-de Silva, B. R., Dodson-Lavelle, B., Raison, C. L., Negi, L. T., Silva, B. R. O., & Phil, D. (2012). Compassion and ethics: Scientific and practical approaches to the cultivation of compassion as a foundation for ethical subjectivity and well-being. *Journal of Healthcare, Science and the Humanities, 2*(1), 145–161.

Parks, A. C., & Schueller, S. (Eds.) (2014). *The Wiley-Blackwell handbook of positive psychological interventions.* Malden, MA: Wiley-Blackwell.

Parnas, J. (2000). The self and intentionality in the pre-psychotic stages of schizophrenia. In D. Zahavi (Ed.), *Exploring the self: Philosophical and psychopathological perspectives on self-experience* (pp. 115–147). Amsterdam: John Benjamins.

Passmore, J., & Theeboom, T. (2016). Coaching psychology research: A journey of development. In L. E. Van Zyl, M. W. Stander & A. Odendaal (Eds.), *Coaching psychology: Meta-theoretical perspectives and applications in multicultural contexts* (pp. 27–46). Cham: Springer.

Pedrotti, J. T., Edwards, L. M., & Lopez, S. J. (2008). Promoting hope: Suggestions for school counselors. *Professional School Counseling, 12,* 100–107.

Peterson, C., & Park, N. (2005). The enduring value of the Boulder Model: Upon this rock we build. *Journal of Clinical Psychology, 61*(9), 1147–1150. DOI:10.1002/jclp.20154.

Peterson, C., & Seligman, M. E. P. (2004). *Character strengths and virtues: A handbook and classification.* New York: Oxford University Press.

Peterson, C., Ruch, W., Beerman, U., Park, N., & Seligman, M. E. P. (2007). Strengths of character, orientations to happiness, and life satisfaction. *Journal of Positive Psychology, 2,* 149–156.

Phelan, J. P. (2012). Forgiveness. *Mindfulness, 3*(3), 254–257. https://doi.org/10.1007/s12671-012-0129-y

Piko, B. F., & Brassai, L. (2009). The role of individual and familial protective factors in adolescents' diet control. *Journal of Health Psychology, 14,* 810–819.

Pritchard, M. E., Wilson, G. S., & Yamnitz, B. (2007). What predicts adjustment among college students? A longitudinal panel study. *Journal of American College Health, 56*(1), 15–22.

Proyer, R., & Ruch, W. (2011). The virtuousness of adult playfulness: The relation of playfulness with strengths of character. *Psychology of Well-being: Theory, Research, and Practice, 1,* article 4. DOI:10.1186/2211-1522-1-4

Qian, X. L., & Yarnal, C. (2011) The role of playfulness in the leisure stress-coping process among emerging adults: A SEM analysis. *Leisure/Loisir, 35*(2), 191–209.

Rashid, T., & Anjum, A. (2011). 340 ways to use VIA character strengths. https://tayyabrashid.com/pdf/via_strengths.pdf

Reichard, B., Avey, J., Lopez, S. J., Dollwet, M., & Marques, S. (2013). Having the will and finding the way: A review and meta-analysis of hope at work. *Journal of Positive Psychology, 8*(4), 292–304.

Reis, H. T., & Rusbult, C. E. (Eds.) (2004). *Close relationships: Key readings in social psychology.* New York: Psychology Press.

Robins, C. J., Keng, S. L., Ekblad, A. G., & Brantley, J. G. (2012). Effects of mindfulness-based stress reduction on emotional experience and expression: A randomized controlled trial. *Journal of Clinical Psychology, 68,* 117–131.

Roepke, A. M., Jayawickreme, E., & Riffle, O. M. (2014). Meaning and health: A systematic review. *Applied Research in Quality of Life, 9,* 1055–1079.

Roth, S., & Cohen, L. J. (1986). Approach, avoidance, and coping with stress. *American Psychologist, 41,* 813–819.

Rotter, J. B. (1966) Generalized expectancies for internal versus external control of reinforcement. *Psychological Monographs: General and Applied, 80*(1), 1–28.

Routledge, C., Arndt, J., Wildschut, T., Sedikides, C., Hart, C. M., Juhl, J., ... & Schlotz, W. (2011). The past makes the present meaningful: Nostalgia as an existential resource. *Journal of Personality and Social Psychology, 101*(3), 638–652.

Runco, M., & Acar, S. (2012). Divergent thinking as a predictor of creative potential. *Creativity Research Journal, 24*(1), 66–75.

Rupp, M. A., Sweetman, R., Sosa, A. E., Smither, J. A., & McConnell, D. S. (2017). Searching for affective and cognitive restoration: Examining the restorative effects of casual video game play. *Human Factors, 59*, 1096–1107.

Ryan, R. M., & Deci, E. L. (2000). Self-determination theory and the facilitation of intrinsic motivation, social development, and wellbeing. *American Psychologist, 55*, 68–78.

Ryan, R. M., & Deci, E. L. (2001). On happiness and human potentials: A review of research on hedonic and eudaimonic well-being. *Annual Review of Psychology, 52*(1), 141–166.

Ryan, R. M., Curren, R. R., & Deci, E. L. (2013). What humans need: Flourishing in Aristotelian philosophy and self-determination theory. In A. S. Waterman (Ed.), *The best within us: Positive psychology perspectives on eudaimonia* (pp. 57–75). Washington, DC: American Psychological Association.

Ryff, C. D. (1989). Happiness is everything, or is it? Explorations on the meaning of psychological well-being. *Journal of Personality and Social Psychology, 57*, 1069–1081.

Schopenhauer, A. ([1840] 1995). *On the basis of morality* (E. F. J. Payne, trans.). New York: Berghahn Books.

Schulz, R., & Heckhausen, J. (1996). A life span model of successful aging. *American Psychologist, 51*, 702–714.

Schulz, R., Hebert, R. S., Dew, M. A., Brown, S. L., Scheier, M. F., Beach, S. R., ... & Langa, K. M. (2007). Patient suffering and caregiver compassion: New opportunities for research, practice, and policy. *The Gerontologist, 47*(1), 4–13. https://doi.org/10.1093/geront/47.1.4

Schwartz, S. (2006). Basic human values: An overview. The Hebrew University of Jerusalem. https://uranos.ch/research/references/Schwartz_2006/Schwartzpaper.pdf

Schwartz, S. (2012). An overview of the Schwartz theory of basic values. *Online Readings in Psychology and Culture, 2*(1). https://doi.org/10.9707/2307-0919.1116

Segal, Z. V., Williams, M. G., & Teasdale, J. D. (2002). *Mindfulness-based cognitive therapy for depression: A new approach to preventing relapse.* New York: Guilford Press.

Segerstrom, S. C., & Miller, G. E. (2004). Psychological stress and the human immune system: A meta-analytic study of 30 years of inquiry. *Psychological Bulletin, 104*, 601–630.

Selcuk, E., Karagobek, A. B., & Gunaydin, G. (2019). Responsiveness as key predictor of happiness: Mechanisms and unanswered questions. In M. Demir & N. Sümer (Eds.), *Close relationships and happiness across cultures, volume 13: Cross-cultural advancements in positive psychology.* New York: Springer.

Seligman, M. E. P. (2002). *Authentic happiness: Using the new positive psychology to realise your potential for lasting fulfilment*. London: Nicholas Brealey Publishing.

Seligman, M. E. P. (2018). *The hope circuit*. North Sydney, NSW: Penguin Random House.

Shapiro, D. H. (1980). *Meditation: Self-regulation strategy and altered states of consciousness*. Chicago, IL: Aldine.

Shapiro, S. L., Carlson, L. E., Astin, J. A., & Freedman, B. (2006). Mechanisms of mindfulness. *Journal of Clinical Psychology, 62*(3), 373–386.

Shapiro, S. L., Schwartz, G. R., & Santerre, C. (2005). Meditation and positive psychology. In C. R. Snyder & S. J. Lopez (Eds.), *Handbook of positive psychology* (pp. 632–645). Oxford: Oxford University Press.

Shapiro, S. L., Walsh, R., & Britton, W. B. (2003). An analysis of recent meditation research and suggestions for future directions. *Journal for Meditation and Meditation Research, 3*, 69–90.

Shek, D. T. L. (1995). Marital quality and psychological well-being of married adults in a Chinese context. *Journal of Genetic Psychology, 156*, 45–56.

Sheldon, K. M., & Elliot, A. J. (1999). Goal striving, need satisfaction, and longitudinal well-being: The self-concordance model. *Journal of Personality and Social Psychology, 76*(3), 482–497.

Shuck, B., Alagaraja, M., Immekus, J., Cumberland, D., & Honeycutt-Elliott, M. (2019). Does compassion matter in leadership? A two-stage sequential equal status mixed method exploratory study of compassionate leader behavior and connections to performance in human resource development. *Human Resource Development Quarterly, 30*(4), 537–564. https://doi.org/https://doi.org/10.1002/hrdq.21369

Siegel, D. (2014). *Brainstorm: The power of the adolescent brain*. London: Penguin.

Siegel, R. D., Germer, C. K., & Olendzki, A. (2009). Mindfulness: What is it? Where does it come from? In F. Didonna (Ed.), *Clinical handbook of mindfulness* (pp. 17–35). New York: Springer.

Sinclair, S., Kondejewski, J., Schulte, F., Letourneau, N., Kuhn, S., Raffin-Bouchal, S., … & Strother, D. (2020). Compassion in pediatric healthcare: A scoping review. *Journal of Pediatric Nursing, 51*, 57–66. https://doi.org/https://doi.org/10.1016/j.pedn.2019.12.009

Sinclair, S., Raffin-Bouchal, S., Venturato, L., Mijovic-Kondejewski, J., & Smith-MacDonald, L. (2017). Compassion fatigue: A meta-narrative review of the healthcare literature. *International Journal of Nursing Studies, 69*, 9–24. https://doi.org/https://doi.org/10.1016/j.ijnurstu.2017.01.003

Skinner, E. A., Edge, K., Altman, J., & Sherwood, H. (2003). Searching for the structure of coping: A review and critique of category systems for classifying ways of coping. *Psychological Bulletin, 129*, 216–269.

Smyth, J. M., Pennebaker, J. W., & Arigo, D. (2012). What are the health effects of disclosure? In A. Baum, T. A. Revenson & J. Singer (Eds.), *Handbook of health psychology* (2nd edn, pp. 175–191). New York: Psychology Press.

Snyder, C. R. (2002). Hope theory: Rainbows in the mind. *Psychological Inquiry*, *13*(4), 249–275.

Snyder, C. R., Feldman, D. B., Shorey, H. S., & Rand, K. L. (2002). Hopeful choices: A school counselor's guide to hope theory. *Professional School Counseling*, *5*(5), 298–307.

Snyder, C. R., Harris, C., Anderson, J. R., Holleran, S. A., Irving, L. M., Sigmon, S. T., & …Harney, P. (1991). The will and the ways: Development and validation of an individual-differences measure of hope. *Journal of Personality and Social Psychology*, *60*(4), 570–585.

Snyder, C. R., Hoza, B., Pelham, W. E., Rapoff, M., Ware, L., Danovsky, M., Highberger, L., Rubinstein, H., & Stahl, K. J. (1997). The development and validation of the Children's Hope Scale. *Journal of Pediatric Psychology*, *22*, 399–421.

Snyder, C. R., Irving, L., & Anderson, J. R. (1991). Hope and health: Measuring the will and the ways. In C. R. Snyder & D. R. Forsyth (Eds.), *Handbook of social and clinical psychology: The health perspective* (pp. 285–305). Elmsford, NY: Pergamon.

Snyder, C. R., Rand, K. L., King, E. A., Feldman, D. B., & Woodward, J. T. (2002). False hope. *Journal of Clinical Psychology*, *58*(9), 1003–1022.

Snyder, C. R., Shorey, H. S., Cheavens, J., Pulvers, K. M., Adams, V. H. III, & Wiklund, C. (2002). Hope and academic success in college. *Journal of Educational Psychology*, *94*(4), 820–826.

Špinka, M., Newberry, R. C., & Bekoff, M. (2001). Mammalian play: Training for the unexpected. *The Quarterly Review of Biology*, *76*, 141–168.

Stahl, B., & Goldstein, E. (2019). *A mindfulness-based stress reduction workbook*. Oakland, CA: New Harbinger Publications.

Stanley, E. A., Schaldach, J. M., Kiyonaga, A., & Jha, A. P. (2011). Mindfulness-based mind fitness training: A case study of a high-stress predeployment military cohort. *Cognitive and Behavioral Practice*, *18*, 566–576.

Steger, M. F., & Frazier, P. (2005). Meaning in life: One link in the chain from religion to well-being. *Journal of Counseling Psychology*, *52*, 574–582.

Steger, M. F., Fitch-Martin, A., Donnelly, J., & Rickard, K. M. (2015). Meaning in life and health: Proactive health orientation links meaning in life to health variables among American undergraduates. *Journal of Happiness Studies*, *16*, 583–597.

Steger, M. F., Frazier, P., Oishi, S., & Kaler, M. (2006). The Meaning in Life questionnaire: Assessing the presence of and search for meaning in life. *Journal of Counseling Psychology*, *53*, 80–93.

Steger, M. F., Frazier, P., & Zacchanini, J. L. (2008a). Terrorism in two cultures: Traumatization and existential protective factors following the September 11th attacks and the Madrid train bombings. *Journal of Trauma and Loss*, *13*, 511–527.

Steger, M. F., Kashdan, T. B., & Oishi, S. (2008b). Being good by doing good: Eudaimonic activity and daily well-being correlates, mediators, and temporal relations. *Journal of Research in Personality*, *42*, 22–42.

Steger, M. F., Kashdan, T. B., Sullivan, B. A., & Lorentz, D. (2008c). Understanding the search for meaning in life: Personality, cognitive style, and the dynamic between seeking and experiencing meaning. *Journal of Personality, 76*, 199–228.

Steger, M. F., Kawabata, Y., Shimai, S., & Otake, K. (2008d). The meaningful life in Japan and the United States: Levels and correlates of meaning in life. *Journal of Research in Personality, 42*, 660–678.

Steger, M. F., Shim, Y., Barenz, J., & Shin, J. Y. (2014). Through the windows of the soul: A pilot study using photography to enhance meaning in life. *Journal of Contextual Behavioral Science, 3*(1), 27–30. https://doi.org/10.1016/j.jcbs.2013.11.002

Sterling, P. (2012). Allostasis: A model of predictive regulation. *Physiology and Behavior, 106*(1): 5–15.

Sterling, P., & Eyer, J. (1988). Allostasis: A new paradigm to explain arousal pathology. In D. Fisher & J. T. Reason (Eds.), *Handbook of life stress, cognition, and health* (pp. 629–649). New York: Wiley.

Sterling, P., & Laughlin, S. (2015). *Principles of neural design.* Cambridge, MA: MIT Press.

Stillman, T. F., Lambert, N. M., Fincham, F. D., & Baumeister, R. F. (2011). Meaning as magnetic force: Evidence that meaning in life promotes interpersonal appeal. *Social Psychological and Personality Science, 2*(1), 13–20.

Sutton-Smith, B. (1997). *The ambiguity of play.* Cambridge, MA: Harvard University Press.

Swann Jr, W. B., Gómez, A., Seyle, D. C., Morales, J., & Huici, C. (2009). Identity fusion: The interplay of personal and social identities in extreme group behavior. *Journal of Personality and Social Psychology, 96*(5), 995–1011. https://doi.org/10.1037/a0013668

Tedeschi, R. G., & Calhoun, L. G. (1995). *Trauma and transformation.* London: Sage.

Tedeschi, R. G., Park, C. L., & Calhoun, L. G. (1998). *Posttraumatic growth: Positive changes in the aftermath of crisis.* Mahwah, NJ: Lawrence Erlbaum.

Tedeschi, R. G., Shakespeare-Finch, J., Taku, K., & Calhoun, L. G. (2018). *Posttraumatic growth theory, research, and applications.* London: Routledge.

Tennen, H., & Affleck, G. (1998). Personality and transformation in the face of adversity. In R. G. Tedeschi, C. L. Park & L. G. Calhoun (Eds.), *Posttraumatic growth: Positive changes in the aftermath of crisis* (pp. 65–98). Mahwah, NJ: Lawrence Erlbaum.

Tillich, P. ([1959] 2014). *The courage to be.* Yale, CT: Yale University Press.

Tunariu, A. D., Tribe, R., Frings, D. J., & Albery, I. P. (2017). The iNEAR programme: An existential positive psychology intervention for resilience and emotional wellbeing. *International Review of Psychiatry, 29*(4), 362–372.

United Nations Development Programme (UNDP) with Charmes, J. (2015). *Time use across the world: Findings of a world compilation of time use surveys.* New York: United Nations.

Valle, M. F., Huebner, E. S., & Suldo, S. M. (2006). An analysis of hope as a psychological strength. *Journal of School Psychology, 44*, 393–406.

van Leeuwen, L., & Westwood, D. (2008). Adult play, psychology and design. *Digital Creativity*, *19*, 153–161.

van Nieuwerburgh, C. (2020). *An introduction to coaching skills: A practical guide* (3rd edn). London: Sage.

van Son, J., Nyklíček, I., Pop, V. J., Blonk, M. C., Erdtsieck, R. J., & Pouwer, F. (2014). Mindfulness-based cognitive therapy for people with diabetes and emotional problems. *Journal of Psychosomatic Research*, *77*, 81–84.

Vansteenkiste, M., Simons, J., Lens, W., Sheldon, K. M., & Deci, E. L. (2004). Motivating learning, performance, and persistence: The synergistic effects of intrinsic goal contents and autonomy-supportive contexts. *Journal of Personality and Social Psychology*, *87*(2), 246–260.

Vaughan, F. (1985). Discovering transpersonal identity. *Journal of Humanistic Psychology*, *25*(3), 13–38.

Vittersø, J. (2011). Recreate or create? Leisure as an arena for recovery and change. In R. Biswas-Diener (Ed.), *Positive psychology as social change* (pp. 293–308). Dordrecht: Springer.

Vittersø, J. (2013). Feelings, meanings, and optimal functioning: Some distinctions between hedonic and eudaimonic well-being. In A. S. Waterman (Ed.), *The best within us: Positive psychology perspectives on eudaimonia* (pp. 39–55). Washington, DC: American Psychological Association.

Vittersø, J., Chipeniuk, R., Skår, M., & Vistad, O. I. (2004) Recreational conflict is affective: The case of cross-country skiers and snowmobiles. *Leisure Sciences*, *26*(3), 227–243.

Vyskocilova, J., Prasko, J., Ociskova, M., Sedlackova, Z., & Mozny, P. (2015). Values and values work in cognitive behavioural therapy. *European Psychiatry*, *57*(1–2), 40–48.

Wagner, L. (2020). Character strengths and PERMA: Investigating the relationships of character strengths with a multidimensional framework of well-being. *Applied Research in Quality of Life*, *15*, 307–328.

Wallace, B. A. (2005). *Balancing the mind*. Boulder, CO: Snow Lion.

Walsh, F. (1998). Beliefs, spirituality, and transcendence: Keys to family resilience. In M. McGoldrick (Ed.), *Re-visioning family therapy: Race, culture, and gender in clinical practice* (pp. 62–77). New York: Guilford Press.

Walsh, F. (2012). Family resilience: Strengths forged through adversity. In *Normal family processes* (4th edn, pp. 399–427). New York: Guilford Press.

Walsh, R. N. (1983). Meditation practice and research. *Journal of Humanistic Psychology*, *23*, 18–50.

Waterman, A. S. (1993). Two conceptions of happiness: Contrasts of personal expressiveness (eudaimonia) and hedonic enjoyment. *Journal of Personality and Social Psychology*, *64*, 678–691.

Weis, R., & Speridakos, E. C. (2011). A meta-analysis of hope enhancement strategies in clinical and community settings. *Psychology of Well-Being: Theory, Research and Practice*, *1*(5), 1–16.

Wellbeing Lab. (2020). The Wellbeing Lab 2020 workplace report: The state of wellbeing in Australian workplaces. www.michellemcquaid.com

Wigger, J. (2018). Invisible friends across four countries: Kenya, Malawi, Nepal and the Dominican Republic. *International Journal of Psychology*, *53*, 46–52.

Williams, C. (2019). The hero's journey: A mudmap for change. *Humanistic Psychology & Research*, *59*(4), 522–539.

Williams, J. M. G., Alatiq, Y., Crane, C., Barnhofer, T., Fennell, M. J. V., Duggan, D. S., Hepburn, S., & Goodwin, G. M. (2008). Mindfulness-based cognitive therapy (MBCT) in bipolar disorder. *Journal of Affective Disorders*, *107*, 275–279.

Winnicott, D. W. (1965/2018). *The maturational process and the facilitating environment*. New York: Routledge.

Wispe, L. (1991). *The psychology of sympathy*. New York: Plenum.

Witek-Janusek, L., Albuquerque, K., Rambo Chroniak, K., Chroniak, C., Durazo-Arvizu, R., & Mathews, H. (2008). Effect of mindfulness-based stress reduction on immune function, quality of life and coping in women newly diagnosed with early stage breast cancer. *Brain, Behavior, and Immunity*, *22*, 969–981.

Witkiewitz, K., Bowen, S., Harrop, E. N., Douglas, H., Enkema, M., & Sedgwick, C. (2014). Mindfulness-based treatment to prevent addictive behavior relapse: Theoretical models and hypothesized mechanisms of change. *Substance Use & Misuse*, *49*, 513–524.

Yıldırım, M., & Arslan, G. (2020). Exploring the associations between resilience, dispositional hope, preventive behaviours, subjective well-being, and psychological health among adults during early stage of COVID-19. *Current Psychology*. https://doi.org/10.1007/s12144-020-01177-2

Zautra, A., Hall, J. S., & Murray, K. E. (2010). *Handbook of adult resilience*. New York: Guilford Press.

Zerubavel, N., & Messman-Moore, T. L. (2013). Staying present: Incorporating mindfulness into therapy for dissociation. *Mindfulness*, *6*(2), 303–314.

Index

Page numbers in **bold** indicate tables.